Entrepreneurial Intensity

Entrepreneurial Intensity

Sustainable Advantages for Individuals, Organizations, and Societies

Michael H. Morris

Foreword by Leyland Pitt

QUORUM BOOKS
Westport, Connecticut • London

Library of Congress Cataloging-in-Publication Data

Morris, Michael H.
   Entrepreneurial intensity : sustainable advantages for
individuals, organizations, and societies / Michael H. Morris; foreword
by Leyland Pitt.
      p.   cm.
   Includes bibliographical references and index.
   ISBN 0-89930-975-5 (alk. paper)
   1. Entrepreneurship.   I. Title.
HB615.M674   1998
338'.04—dc21   97-31518

British Library Cataloguing in Publication Data is available.

Library of Congress Catalog Card Number: 97-31518
ISBN: 0-89930-975-5

First published in 1998

Quorum Books, 88 Post Road West, Westport, CT 06881
An imprint of Greenwood Publishing Group, Inc.

Printed in the United States of America

The paper used in this book complies with the
Permanent Paper Standard issued by the National
Information Standards Organization (Z39.48–1984).

10 9 8 7 6 5

Copyright Acknowledgments

The author and publisher are grateful for permission to reproduce portions of the following copyrighted material:

Table 3.1, "Criteria for Evaluating Opportunities," from J.A. Timmons, *New Venture Creation: Entrepreneurship in the 1990s* (Homewood, IL: Irwin, 1990). Copyright 1990. Reprinted with permission of The McGraw-Hill Companies.

Figure 4.2, " 'Missing the Boat' and 'Sinking the Boat' Risk," from "Missing the Boat and Sinking the Boat: A Conceptual Model of Entrepreneurial Risk." Reprinted with permission from *Journal of Marketing,* published by the American Marketing Association, Peter R. Dickson and Joseph J. Giglierano, Vol. 50 (July 1986), 64.

Table 5.1, "Selected Findings on the Role of Environmental Conditions in Facilitating Entrepreneurship," from D.R. Gnyawali and D.S. Fogel, "Environments for Entrepreneurship Development: Key Dimensions and Research Implications," *Entrepreneurship: Theory and Practice,* 18(4) (1994), 47–49. Reprinted with permission.

Figure 7.1, "Key Business Dimensions and Entrepreneurship," from H. Stevenson, M.J. Roberts, and H.I. Grousbeck, *New Business Ventures and the Entrepreneur,* 4th ed. (Burr Ridge, IL: Irwin, 1994). Permission to reproduce granted by Harvard Business School Publishing, August 1997.

To Minet

Entrepreneur, Scholar, Partner, Friend

Contents

Illustrations

FIGURES

Foreword

In a recent *Harvard Business Review* article, Amar Bhide writes lucidly about the questions every entrepreneur must answer. These include

- What kind of enterprise do I need to build?
- What risks and sacrifices does such an enterprise demand?
- Can I accept those risks and sacrifices?
- Is the strategy well defined?
- Can the strategy generate sufficient profits and growth?
- Is the strategy sustainable?
- Are my goals for growth too conservative or too aggressive?
- Do I have the right resources and relationships?
- How strong is the organization?

He goes on to emphasize that the problems entrepreneurs confront every day would overwhelm most managers. Not least among these problems, in my opinion, would be how to answer the questions Bhide poses. While they seem quite straightforward and simple, they lie at the very heart of entrepreneurship itself.

This book will facilitate the answering of these questions by scholars, teachers, researchers, and managers, and most importantly, by entrepreneurs themselves. In it, Michael Morris demonstrates conclusively that entrepreneurship is a process characterized by innovation, proactive behavior, and the willingness to assume risk. All of these attributes are critical to the well-being of our societies today, yet in so many aspects of everyday life they are sorely lacking. In my opinion, the most important contribution of the book is that Morris convinces the reader that entrepreneurship is not just something that small start-up business firms do, but rather that it should be a pervasive facet of our lives. In large and small firms, in for-profit and nonprofit organizations, and in government itself, the entrepreneurial spirit lives, unstifled by bureaucracy, indifference, and comfort.

Entrepreneurship is in danger of becoming another popular "buzzword," loosely applied by consultants, government officials, managers, and others to describe all manner of activity. People use the term "entrepreneurial" to describe potential they see in their children, a job category, departments in their companies, an approach to solving a problem, the strategies their competitors are using, great leaders they admire, countries they have visited, and many other things. Morris moves us beyond the vague conceptualizations and the popular myths. He demonstrates that entrepreneurship is a measurable phenomenon, and that people, companies, and nations should have strategies for managing the role that entrepreneurship will play in their futures. His concept of entrepreneurial intensity (EI) enables us to apply entrepreneurship in specific contexts and to continually enhance the levels of EI that are achieved.

The text is written with all the scholarly rigor one would expect from an outstanding researcher, scholar, and teacher. Yet the spirit of the entrepreneur shines through, and the book is eminently readable. If you are a manager in a large or small organization, I know that you will find a whole host of practical ideas to apply. If you are a researcher in the general field of management, or in entrepreneurship particularly, I expect that you will exploit this text as a valuable scholarly resource. If you are an entrepreneur, I trust that you will find yourself constantly testing ideas against the contents of the book. And if you are a student of entrepreneurship, I hope that you will learn both passively and actively from it.

Michael Morris is a researcher whose work has appeared in the premier journals of his various disciplines. He is a teacher who has classes with students ranging from undergraduates through MBAs to hardened executives on the edges of their seats with his enthusiasm and style. He is also an entrepreneur. He brings these talents to life once more in the pages of this book.

Leyland Pitt
Professor of Marketing and Strategy
Cardiff Business School
University of Wales
Cardiff, United Kingdom

Preface

It has been said that we live in the "age of entrepreneurship." One tends to wonder exactly what this means. Entrepreneurship has actually been with us for a very long time. History is filled with stories of great entrepreneurs who created significant change and built sizable empires. Economists have focused on the concept for well over 200 years. Many courses have been offered and books published that address the subject. So, what is different today?

Obviously, one difference is that the amount of entrepreneurial activity the world over is at unprecedented levels. The number of business start-ups, patents granted, new products and services, technological process improvements, and new organizational forms being introduced is clearly at an all-time high, with reason to believe it will only get higher. And this activity knows no geographic boundaries. With the fall of communism and the opening up of free trade around the world, there is an explosion of entrepreneurship in country after country. The beauty of the current entrepreneurship is that it is also quite democratic. It knows no limitations in terms of the age, race, gender, IQ, cultural background, or politics of the people who make it happen. We find it coming from the most unusual quarters, with everyone from 80-year-old grandmothers to formerly virulent anti-capitalists creating new ventures. And we find entrepreneurial behavior applied in firms small and large, as well as in non-profit organizations, political movements, and even government agencies.

But the age of entrepreneurship is defined by much more than an increase in activity. It represents a fundamental change in our way of thinking about business, life, and the environments in which we find ourselves. This new way of thinking centers around the concepts of individual responsibility and personal choice.

Let's first consider the individual. The age of entrepreneurship is one in which we focus on the microcosm before the macrocosm, where approaches are bottom-up not top-down, and small units in alliance consistently outdo large organizations that rely on scale and control. Words like devolution, downsizing, decentralization, and empowerment attempt to capture this movement away from the concentrated center to the diverse individual. Entrepreneurship today involves a recognition that people can affect change in their environments and are ultimately responsible for the course that their lives take. Each of us has innate entrepreneurial potential, and each of us can make a meaningful difference in our neighborhoods, schools, workplaces, volunteer efforts, and social encounters. However, we can only do so by taking personal responsibility for change, contribution, and improvement.

Just as critical is the need to recognize that, while the individual is both a valued and respected player in the entrepreneurial age, he/she represents the means rather than the ends. Entrepreneurship is not about self-aggrandizement, hero worship, or greed. It is about individuals who are able to build, share with, motivate, and grow teams of other individuals. Jointly, they create value where there was none. They do so by putting together resources in a slightly (and sometimes significantly) different way than anyone before them. Their willingness to dream and to act on those dreams is not limited by the resources they currently control.

The age of entrepreneurship is also an age of choice. Entrepreneurs have created many of these choices, and their survival today depends on their ability to continually expand and enhance these choices for society's members. Any choice in life (e.g., products, schools, jobs, partners, social encounters, religions) involves a risk-reward trade-off. Entrepreneurship is about recognizing choices for what they are, finding the opportunity in the choices that come along, creating choices where there appear to be none to make, and learning from each and every choice that we make, regardless of the outcome.

This means that entrepreneurship is no longer something that we do at a point in time. It represents a guiding philosophy as well as a behavioral process that can be managed throughout our lives. As a philosophy, the concern is with a consciousness of, and respect for, opportunity, innovation, calculated risk-taking, and tolerance of failure. Behaviorally, there is a need for each of us to develop a personal strategy for determining how much entrepreneurship should be demonstrated at different points in time and in different settings or situations.

The title of this book, *Entrepreneurial Intensity*, is meant to capture this new age of entrepreneurship. The word "intensity" refers to something that is highly concentrated; has a high degree of strength, force or energy; or is strongly emphasized. Entrepreneurial intensity (EI) refers to strength or force of entrepreneurship at three levels: in our individual lives, in the lives of the organizations that we create or join, and throughout our societies. The central thesis of this book is that entrepreneurship occurs in varying degrees and amounts, and that environments can be created in ways that heighten EI at all three levels. It is my sincere wish that in these pages the reader discovers a new relevance

for entrepreneurial thinking, dreaming, acting, doing, and being. Further, I hope that the framework, models, and concepts proposed herein provide a kind of broad blueprint for applying that entrepreneurial thinking and doing to the entire panorama of life's experiences.

1

Common Myths Regarding Entrepreneurship

INTRODUCTION

This book is about entrepreneurship, a subject that has certainly come into vogue in recent years. Governments are trying to foster it, individuals are attempting to practice it in unprecedented numbers, and large organizations are desperately seeking to recapture it. In response, there has been a dramatic increase in the number of schools and universities around the world that are teaching courses in entrepreneurship, with many of them establishing entire programs on the subject. Similarly, the number of books, academic journals, and magazines devoted to the topic has exploded in the past decade.

In the pages that follow, we will attempt to explore various aspects of entrepreneurship, establish why entrepreneurship matters, and discuss how it can be encouraged. As will become apparent, entrepreneurship is a field containing many open controversies and unresolved issues. Considerable disagreement surrounds even such basic questions as the definition of the word "entrepreneurship." This might seem surprising, given that entrepreneurship as an academic or intellectual concept has been around for well over two hundred years. We will put forward a number of perspectives and ideas regarding these issues, while also inviting the reader to develop his/her own opinions.

As a beginning point, it may be helpful to address some of the many misconceptions that people seem to have about entrepreneurship. A number of myths continue to influence the way people think about the topic. These misunderstandings can lead to serious mistakes on the part of would-be entrepreneurs, executives attempting to stimulate the spirit of entreprenurship within established companies, and public policy makers seeking to facilitate entrepreneurial behavior at the societal level. Below, we have identified thirteen key myths or misconceptions and attempted to explain the reality that lies behind each of them.

MYTH 1: ENTREPRENEURSHIP IS ABOUT STARTING AND RUNNING A SMALL BUSINESS

Not necessarily. Entrepreneurship represents a *growth-oriented* outlook. It implies an *innovative* and *proactive* approach to challenges, tasks, needs, obstacles, and opportunities. Many small firms are not very entrepreneurial and can be considered "mom and pop" type operations. For most of these businesses, the only entrepreneurial thing they ever do is open up in the first place. They then become fairly stagnant, complacent, status quo operations. While they do serve an important purpose in the economy, they do not provide much dynamism.

Consider the owner of a dry cleaners located within a strip shopping center in a local suburb. If you ask this individual where he will be in five years, the honest answer is, "I'll be right here. I'm not getting rich but we get by. I don't have to work for anyone else; I employ a family member or two; my boy works here during his summer breaks; and we take a vacation every couple of years." Now, consider the person in the same circumstances who is asked the same question but produces a strategic plan that lays out an inventive franchising and financing concept that he/she has come up with. This person explains, "I have streamlined and standardized my operations and plan to have fifteen of these dry cleaners around the local area in two years, and 150 of them located throughout the region within five years." It is this second person who more closely reflects the entrepreneurial spirit.

Table 1.1 represents a summary of key differences between conventional small businesses and more highly entrepreneurial firms. At the same time, it is dangerous to draw this distinction too finely, for reasons expounded upon in misconception three, below.

Instead, our perspective in this book is that entrepreneurship is a universal construct that is applicable to any person, organization (private or public, large or small), or nation. A growing body of evidence suggests that an entrepreneurial orientation is critical for the survival and growth of companies as well as for the economic prosperity of nations. The need for entrepreneurship is greatest where there are diminishing opportunity streams, as well as rapid changes in technology, consumer needs, industry and market structures, social values, and political roles. In addition, where decision-makers are confronted with short decision windows, unpredictable resource needs, and a lack of long-term control over the environment, entrepreneurship becomes vital.

MYTH 2: ENTREPRENEURSHIP IS A DISCRETE EVENT THAT JUST "HAPPENS"

Entrepreneurship is not a fixed event that occurs at a particular point in time. There is a dynamic process involved, and this process takes time to unfold. The

Table 1.1
Differences between Typical Small Businesses and Entrepreneurial Ventures

Characteristics of Many Small Businesses	Characteristics of Entrepreneurial Ventures
Stable	Unstable
Status quo-oriented	Change-oriented
Not aggressive	More aggressive
Socially-oriented	Commercially-oriented
Interaction between personal and professional activities	Clear separation of personal and professional activities
Involvement of family members	Involvement of professionals
More informal	More formal
Tactical	Strategic
Present-oriented	Future-oriented
Preference for low-risk/low-return activities	Preference for high-risk/high-return activities
Internally oriented	Externally oriented
Steady number of employees	Growing employee base with high potential for conflicts
Level resource needs	Expanding resource needs with ongoing cash shortages
Resource-driven	Opportunity-driven
Concerned with personal profit, income substitution	Concerned with growth and appreciation of business value

process has specific, identifiable stages, starting with the identification of an opportunity and ending with the ultimate success or failure of an implemented concept. As a process, entrepreneurship can be managed. This is a critical point, for the more we recognize that the steps, or stages, are manageable, the more the mystique surrounding entrepreneurship begins to disappear. Further, the process nature of entrepreneurship means that it can be applied in organizations of all sizes and types. The typical entrepreneurial idea undergoes significant modification as it evolves through the process. Getting it through the process requires persistence and patience, aggressiveness, and adaptability.

MYTH 3: ENTREPRENEURSHIP IS AN "EITHER/OR" THING

People seem to approach entrepreneurship in "black and white" terms. Someone is either an entrepreneur, or they are not. Similarly, a company is either thought to be entrepreneurial or not. We place people and organizations into boxes, drawing absolute distinctions between a manager and an entrepreneur, between an entrepreneurial enterprise and a bureaucratic company.

In the real world, entrepreneurship happens in different amounts, and in varying degrees. Every person and every organization does entrepreneurial things at one time or another. Some do them more (versus less) often, and some do things that are more (versus less) innovative. The key is to recognize that entrepreneurship is a *variable* phenomenon.

MYTH 4: ENTREPRENEURSHIP IS ABOUT TAKING WILD RISKS

It is popular to think of entrepreneurs as "gamblers," who are willing to "bet the farm." They seize an opportunity and passionately go after it, throwing caution to the wind. The truth is entrepreneurs are *not* wild-eyed risk-takers. They are willing to assume risks but not unnecessary ones. In fact, their risk profile does not tend to differ statistically all that much from society at large. The difference is, they are *calculated* risk-takers. They will carefully analyze and evaluate a situation. They systematically identify the key financial, technical, market, and other specific risk factors. They then go about identifying ways to manage and minimize the likelihood of any of the underlying risk factors occurring.

Successful entrepreneurs are also good at sharing risks by involving partners, leveraging resources, leasing instead of owning, borrowing instead of buying, and contracting instead of hiring. The entrepreneur is not preoccupied with controlling lots of assets or using only his/her own resources. He/she is not into status or power but only wants to do what is necessary to turn a dream, or vision, into reality.

MYTH 5: ENTREPRENEURS ARE BORN

People also get caught up in the personality cult that surrounds entrepreneurship. We think of the Richard Bransons, Ted Turners, Akio Moritos, and Bill Gateses of the world and associate entrepreneurship with some superhuman class of individuals who are somehow different from the rest of us. After literally hundreds of studies on the psychological and sociological makeup of the entrepreneur, one conclusion emerges—entrepreneurs are not a unique and separate group that is somehow genetically predisposed to be entrepreneurial. They are not born. Rather, we all have some degree of entrepreneurial potential within us. The ability to develop and realize that potential is very much a function of one's environment.

One has only to consider the finding that children who have entrepreneurial role models earlier in life are more likely to do something entrepreneurial than are those who do not have such role models. Similarly, why is there so much more entrepreneurship per capita in some countries (e.g., the United States, Taiwan) than right next door in neighboring countries (e.g., Mexico, China)? The truth is that entrepreneurs are made by learning and experience. Entrepreneurship has much less to do with the gene pool, and much more to do with the family, school, social, and work environments to which individuals are exposed. The making of an entrepreneur depends on the accumulation of activities, skills, and knowledge over time and includes large doses of self-development.

MYTH 6: ENTREPRENEURSHIP IS ABOUT GREED

We've all heard about the entrepreneur who wants to be a millionaire by age 30 and retired by age 40, but it just doesn't work that way. Even for those few who are rich and retired at 40, the probability is quite high that, at 41, they are right back at it, pursuing some new opportunity. The real motivator behind entrepreneurial behavior is not money, and it certainly is not power or position. Entrepreneurial individuals tend to be driven by a desire to achieve, to make a difference, to do what others said could not be done, to overcome all the obstacles and naysayers.

This is not to suggest that they don't like money. At least for entrepreneurs in the private sector, financial returns play an important role. They serve as a source of feedback, letting the entrepreneur know that progress is being made. Entrepreneurial events are ambiguous and take time to unfold. The tremendous uncertainty, especially in the early stages, can lead the entrepreneur to question himself/herself, the validity of the concept, and whether it is all worth it. Rewards are like road markers, letting the entrepreneur know that he/she is on the right path and is moving towards his/her destination.

MYTH 7: ENTREPRENEURSHIP IS ABOUT INDIVIDUALS

Entrepreneurial events usually have a driving force behind them in the form of a visionary individual, who assumes risk and persists in making change happen. Even in corporate settings, there must be a champion who keeps a new concept alive and sells the organization on it. By definition, entrepreneurship implies a degree of individual autonomy and a sense of personal ownership of an innovative concept. Innovation rarely involves a democratic process.

But entrepreneurship does not happen without teams. Not only is the existence of a team critical, but so too is the quality of the team. Too much must be done to bring a concept to reality, and no one individual has either the time or the talent to do it all well. The obstacles are formidable and the technical, legal, financial, marketing, managerial and administrative requirements are complex.

The challenge is to balance the need for individual initiative with the spirit of cooperation and group ownership of innovation. This balance occurs over the stages of the entrepreneurial process. Individuals are needed to provide the vision, unwavering commitment, and internal salesmanship without which nothing could be accomplished. But as the process unfolds, the entrepreneur requires teams of people with unique skills and resources. These teams may be formal or ad hoc, and their membership is likely to be fluid as people join or depart depending on the venture's requirements. Moreover, the members of the team do more than provide functional expertise or perform specific tasks. They modify and adapt the innovation as new and unanticipated obstacles arise, all the while being kept on track and spurred on by the entrepreneurial champion. They bring to the task a spirit of camaraderie and a sense of being a part of something important. In the final analysis, it is important that this amorphous group take ownership of, and credit for, the end-product.

MYTH 8: THERE IS ONLY ONE TYPE OF ENTREPRENEUR

There is no single prototype of the entrepreneur. They come from all walks of life and represent a diverse mix of age groups, races, religions, cultures, genders, and occupational backgrounds. Some do entrepreneurial things all of their lives, while others pursue some highly entrepreneurial opportunity only after spending a relatively conservative career in some large bureaucratic company.

At the same time, researchers have noted the existence of general categories of entrepreneurs (see Table 1.2). For instance, a distinction has been drawn between *craftsmen* entrepreneurs, who tend to have a fairly narrow educational background, limited social awareness, a limited time orientation, and demonstrate a tendency to create fairly rigid ventures, and *opportunistic* entrepreneurs, who often have a broader educational and social background, are more socially confident and future-oriented, and tend to create more adaptive, growth-oriented enterprises (Smith and Miner, 1983). Another identified category consists of

Table 1.2
Different Categories of Entrepreneurs Identified by Researchers

Author	Categories
Smith (1967)	Craftsmen Entrepreneurs
	Opportunistic Entrepreneurs
Smith (1967) and Kets de Vries (1977)	R&D/Technical/Inventor Entrepreneurs
Vesper (1980)	Solo Self-Employed
	Team Builders
	Independent Innovators
	Pattern Multipliers
	Economy of Scale Exploiters
	Acquirers
	Buy-Sell Artists
	Conglomerators
	Apparent Value Manipulators
Kao (1991)	Creative/Charismatic Entrepreneurs
	Conventional Entrepreneurs
Miner (1996)	Personal Achievers
	Supersalespeople
	Real Managers
	Expert Idea Generators

technical/inventor entrepreneurs. These are people with strong technical backgrounds, who often have worked in a research and development or related position within a large organization and start a venture based on some invention, technology application, or new process that they have designed.

More recently, in a landmark study by Miner (1996), four major types of entrepreneurs were identified based on extensive research: the *personal achiever*, the *supersalesperson*, the *real manager*, and the *expert idea generator*. Personal achievers are classic entrepreneurs, with lots of initiative, strong commitment, and a strong internal locus of control (sense of their ability to affect change in their external environment). They like feedback about their performance and enjoy planning and goal setting for future achievements. Supersalespeople demonstrate a great deal of feeling for, and a desire to help, other people. They are very good at the soft sell and external relationship building, while letting others handle the administrative details of running the business. Real managers like power and taking charge. They often come from a large corporate background, are competitive and decisive, employ the hard sell, and are good at building an existing business into something much larger. Expert idea generators build a venture around new products, niches, or processes that they have been involved with inventing. They are often involved with high-tech companies.

MYTH 9: ENTREPRENEURSHIP REQUIRES LOTS OF MONEY

Entrepreneurial individuals are opportunity-driven, not resource-driven. They do not limit the scope of their vision by how much money, time, staff, or related resources they own. Rather, they go after their dream by leveraging resources—by borrowing, begging, partnering, sharing, leasing and recycling resources. And it's not just financial resources. Studies of entrepreneurial failure suggest that the problem far more often is related not to money, but to other resources, such as poorly prepared managers, inadequate distribution channels, or ill-conceived marketing efforts.

While people tend to associate entrepreneurship with coming up with creative business concepts, the reality is that lots of us come up with novel ideas for a new product or service but never do anything about it. In many instances, the truly entrepreneurial behavior comes into play in identifying usable resources and finding ways to acquire them without necessarily buying them outright. Also, good entrepreneurs manage to get more out of less when it comes to resources. They often move ahead without all of the requisite resources and fill in the gaps as opportunities arise.

MYTH 10: ENTREPRENEURSHIP IS ABOUT LUCK

No, entrepreneurs tend to create their own "luck." It's much more about hard work, creative insight, in-depth analysis, adaptability, and an openness to opportunity when it comes along. The evidence suggests there is no best way to generate new ideas and concepts. However, entrepreneurs are more externally-than internally-focused, more opportunity- than resource-driven. In addition, experience is a vital factor.

The entrepreneurial individual recognizes a pattern—a trend, a possibility, an incongruity, an unmet need—when it is still taking shape. These patterns consist of recognizable pieces that can be adapted from one context to another and then put together. They are rooted in the market, and more specifically, in such factors as customer needs, customer problems, buying behavior, limitations of current products, and assumptions made by competitors. Further, the ability to link knowledge of technology, familiarity with distribution channels, awareness of regulatory and legal restrictions, and an understanding of the capabilities of suppliers to these aspects of the market is what typically produces brilliant and successful entrepreneurship. Entrepreneurs come up with unique concepts for capitalizing on a trend or need and do so while the window of opportunity is open. They put themselves in the right place at the right time and are fully aware of the downside chances of failure.

MYTH 11: ENTREPRENEURSHIP STARTS WITH A NEW PRODUCT OR SERVICE

This is one of the great mistakes many would-be entrepreneurs make. They come up with a novel product concept without ever determining whether a need exists, how extensive that need actually is, how satisfied customers are with current products, what their switching costs would be, and whether they will be able to see meaningful advantages in the new product. Entrepreneurship does not start with the product or service one would like to sell. It starts with an opportunity, and opportunities are rooted in the external environment.

There is an old adage, ''If you build a better mousetrap, the world will beat a path to your door.'' The greater likelihood is that the grass will grow tall on the pathway to your door unless

- the mousetrap is targeted to the right audience,
- that audience is sufficiently large,
- the audience is sufficiently unhappy with, and not loyal to, the product they are using now,
- distributors exist who are willing to carry the mousetrap given their current product assortment and supplier agreements,
- the technology used in making the mousetrap is not likely to become outdated any time soon,
- competitors are not likely to introduce a better or cheaper version of the mousetrap a month from now,

- economic conditions do not exist that make, or will make, the mousetrap unaffordable, and

- new safety regulations are not on the horizon that will force a redesign in the mousetrap to bring it into compliance.

This is but a sample of environmental factors that can spell defeat for even the most innovative new products or services.

It is easy to get very excited about any new concept. The problem is that the people who come up with these ideas often suffer from a kind of "entrepreneurial myopia." They are preoccupied with the product (and keeping it a secret), as well as with all the start-up obstacles and issues that they face. As a result, they just assume that a market need exists, that suppliers and distributors are readily available, and that environmental conditions will remain as they are now.

MYTH 12: ENTREPRENEURSHIP IS UNSTRUCTURED AND CHAOTIC

There is also a tendency to think of entrepreneurs as gunslingers—as people who shoot from the hip and ask questions later. They are assumed by some to be disorganized and unstructured, leaving it to others to keep things on track. The reality is that entrepreneurs are heavily involved in all facets of their venture, and they usually have a number of balls in the air at the same time. As a result, they are typically well-organized individuals. They tend to have a system, perhaps elaborate, perhaps not, but personally designed to keep things straight and maintain priorities. In fact, their system may seem strange to the casual observer, but it works.

When doing something entrepreneurial, one is dealing with the unknown, and there is a need to be tolerant of ambiguity. Unanticipated developments arise all the time. Success is often a function of how prepared one is for the unknown, and how much one is in a position to capitalize on the unanticipated. The entrepreneur's ability to meet daily and weekly obligations, while also growing the venture, and while also being able to move quickly when novel events occur, is strongly affected by his/her organizing capabilities. Plans, outlines, forecasts, checklists, timetables, budgets, databases, and pert charts are examples of tools that the contemporary entrepreneur always keeps close at hand.

MYTH 13: MOST ENTREPRENEURIAL VENTURES FAIL

Many do, but many do not. Failure rates differ widely by industry, ranging from as low as 10% to as high as 90%. Further, they drop off significantly after the first few years of operation. And yet, entrepreneurship is about making change happen. People (customers, managers in established companies, bankers, suppliers, distributors, regulators) naturally resist change. Thus, in any entrepreneurial effort, there will be all of the natural obstacles, plus all of the arbitrary obstacles that people throw in one's path. Failure becomes a normal by-product of entrepreneurial effort. It is the number-one way in which an entrepreneur learns what works and does not work. He/she then determines the reasons why and makes the adjustments necessary to fight another day.

It is also important to keep in mind that failure rates rise as the amount of entrepreneurial activity rises. One has only to consider the high failure rates experienced by new restaurants. Many of these fail because they are not well-positioned, the target market is not well-defined, or the restaurant fails to adequately differentiate itself. However, the failure rate is especially high because the number of start-ups is high. The same goes for bankruptcy. Some observers read a newspaper headline that says the bankruptcy rate is at an all-time high and interpret this as bad news. But bankruptcy rates are high because the new business start-up rate is also at an all-time high.

So, failure rates are likely to go up in the coming years as the number of new products introduced and new businesses started goes up. The likelihood of failure can be significantly reduced, however, by planning for, and systematically managing, the stages in the entrepreneurial process.

CONCLUSIONS

One might wonder why myths such as the ones outlined in this chapter continue to persist. The answer is that, while we tend to encounter entrepreneurship all around us, brushing up against it in all facets of our lives, there really is no "discipline of entrepreneurship." That is, unlike chemistry or physics or accounting, entrepreneurship is not really a formal discipline. It is a cross-disciplinary pursuit, involving bits of psychology, finance, engineering, sociology, marketing, physics, management, mathematics, and economics.

As an area of serious intellectual endeavor, most of the substantive research on entrepreneurship has been done during this century, and much of it in the past 30 years. As a result, there is no universal theory of entrepreneurship, and most of the theories one does find in the research are borrowed from other disciplines. It is difficult to talk of "paradigm shifts" in the field, for the paradigms themselves have yet to be clearly defined. Few laws, principles, or established concepts exist to guide the efforts of academics or practitioners who are attempting to better understand the phenomenon of entrepreneurship. Further, much of the published research is qualitative in nature, which makes it very difficult to draw generalizable conclusions.

Yet, entrepreneurship makes great headlines. The success stories of people like Ray Kroc of MacDonald's, Sochiro Honda of Honda Motors, or Herb Kelleher of Southwest Airlines are nothing short of inspirational. And when some entrepreneur gets into serious ethical or legal trouble, as John Delorean and his controversial automobile did a few years back, that also receives a lot of attention. As stories are told and retold regarding these heroes and anti-heroes, a mythology is created.

However, entrepreneurship is mostly about simple people with simple dreams. As we have seen, the practical requirements of turning these dreams into realities are quite far removed from many of the myths and misconceptions. In the chapters that follow, we will examine a number of these issues in much more detail. We begin first by exploring the controversies surrounding the definition of entrepreneurship.

REFERENCES

Kao, J.J. 1991. *The Entrepreneur*. Englewood Cliffs, N.J.: Prentice-Hall.

Kets de Vries, M.F.R. 1977. "The Entrepeneurial Personality: A Person at the Crossroads." *Journal of Management Studies*, 14 (1), 34–57.

Miner, J.B. 1996. *The 4 Routes to Entrepreneurial Success*. San Francisco: Berrett-Koehler Publishers.

Ronstadt, R.C. 1985. *Entrepreneurship: Text, Cases and Notes*. Dover: Lord Publishing.

Smith, N.R. 1967. *The Entrepreneur and His Firm: The Relationship between Type of Man and Type of Company*. East Lansing: Bureau of Business and Economic Research, Graduate School of Business Administration, Michigan State University.

Smith, N.R., and Miner, J.B. 1983. "Type of Entrepreneur, Type of Firm, and Managerial Motivation: Implications for Organizational Life Cycle Theory." *Strategic Management Journal*, 4 (4), 325–340.

Stevenson, H.H., Roberts, M.J., and Grousbeck, H.I. 1994. *New Business Venture and the Entrepreneur*. Homewood, IL: Irwin.

Timmons, J.A. 1990. *New Venture Creation: Entrepreneurship in the 1990s*. Homewood, IL: Irwin.

2

Understanding Entrepreneurship

INTRODUCTION

The significant amount of attention devoted to entrepreneurship in recent years has resulted in a keen awareness of the limitations of current knowledge on the subject. For instance, various critiques of the available literature note the lack of a well-defined research agenda or set of research programs in the entrepreneurship field and conclude that most of the contemporary research lacks clarity and consensus regarding purpose, theoretical perspective, focus, level of analysis, time frame, and methodology.

A more fundamental concern is the general lack of agreement among scholars and practitioners regarding the nature of entrepreneurship itself. A wide variety of definitions can be found in even the most recent literature, and conflicting schools of thought continue to debate the relative importance of various underlying dimensions and to disagree about the distinction between a small business and an entrepreneurial venture.

In this chapter, we attempt to provide a unified conceptualization regarding the nature and scope of entrepreneurship. A distinction is drawn between inputs to, and outputs from, the entrepreneurial process. It is argued that entrepreneurship is a variable phenomenon that can be characterized in terms of its intensity. An integrative model is presented that relates entrepreneurial input, process, intensity, and output. It is argued that the model can be applied at the level of the individual, the organization, or society.

THE DEFINITION OF ENTREPRENEURSHIP

Historical Perspectives

Although the term "entrepreneurship" has been used in a business context for well over 200 years, there is still considerable disagreement about its meaning. While there have been literally hundreds of perspectives, seven of the most prevalent themes are summarized in Table 2.1.

Early definitions, which were formulated principally by economists, tended to emphasize assumption of risk, supply of financial capital, arbitrage, and coordination of the factors of production. While the entrepreneur was clearly involved in the initiation of a business, these early perspectives saw entrepreneurship as an ongoing function in companies, and profit as a return for addressing uncertainty and coordinating resources. Economists historically failed to make a distinction between management and entrepreneurship or to address the differences between small and large firms. In fact, distinctions like these were not well established until the 1930's. Even so, the prevalent tendency has been to associate entrepreneurship with small business start-up and management. As such, the entrepreneur has been viewed as someone who assumes the social, psychological, and financial risks necessary to start and run a small business (Hisrich and Peters, 1992).

Based on the work of Schumpeter and others in the first half of the twentieth century, the central focus shifted to innovation, or carrying out unique combi-

Table 2.1
Seven Perspectives on the Nature of Entrepreneurship

Creation of Wealth	Entrepreneurship involves assuming the risks associated with the facilitation of production in exchange for profit.
Creation of Enterprise	Entrepreneurship entails the founding of a new business venture where none existed before.
Creation of Innovation	Entrepreneurship is concerned with unique combinations of resources that make existing methods or products obsolete.
Creation of Change	Entrepreneurship involves creating change by adjusting, adapting, and modifying one's personal repertoire, approaches, and skills to meet different opportunities available in the environment.
Creation of Employment	Entrepreneurship is concerned with employing, managing, and developing the factors of production, including the labor force.
Creation of Value	Entrepreneurship is a process of creating value for customers by exploiting untapped opportunities.
Creation of Growth	Entrepreneurship is defined as a strong and positive orientation towards growth in sales, income, assets, and employment.

nations of resources in order to create new products, services, processes, organizational structures, sources of supply, and markets (Schumpeter, 1934). Entrepreneurs were engaged in an activity labelled "creative destruction," where they continually made existing methods and products obsolete by successfully introducing innovations. An extension of the Schumpeterian perspective is to identify entrepreneurship as a principal agent of change in society (Tropman and Morningstar, 1989).

More recently, there has been an attempt to distinguish the entrepreneur from entrepreneurship. The traits and characteristics that distinguish entrepreneurs from both managers and society-at-large was a favored research topic in the late 1970's and early 1980's (e.g., Brockhaus and Horwitz, 1985). The entrepreneur has been characterized in terms of such psychological traits as achievement motivation, internal locus of control, calculated risk-taking, tolerance of ambiguity, and persistence. Similarly, sociological characteristics, such as being first in the family birth order, being an immigrant, and having early role models, have been associated with the entrepreneurial personality. While the findings and implications of this stream of research remain controversial, attention has moved from examining the person to examining the process.

Conceptualizing entrepreneurship as a process that occurs in an organizational setting has significantly advanced the field, with considerable attention devoted to describing the steps or stages involved and identifying factors that both constrain and facilitate the process. Although the process has been described in various ways, it generally consists of the stages involved in moving from identifying opportunity to defining a business concept, assessing resource requirements, acquiring those resources, and managing and harvesting the venture (Stevenson et al., 1989).

Approached as a process, entrepreneurship could be applied to organizations of all sizes and types, according to a number of researchers in the 1980's (Brandt, 1986; Kao, 1989; Pinchot, 1985). In fact, a number of the benchmarking studies of corporate excellence suggested that the best-run companies tended to be more entrepreneurial than their competitors in the same or other industries. To the extent that this is true, the distinction between management and entrepreneurship again became unclear. Moreover, some observers began to distinguish entrepreneurial from nonentrepreneurial firms, concluding that many small firms were not especially entrepreneurial.

There has also been a tendency to associate entrepreneurship with the creation of employment (Hornaday and Aboud, 1971). Studies by Birch (1979) and others have demonstrated that entrepreneurial firms are responsible for creating a disproportionate number of the new jobs in the economy. Recent years have witnessed a related conceptualization, in this case emphasizing growth. Growth in this context refers to a significant increase in sales, profits, assets, employees, and sometimes locations. The entrepreneurial firm is defined as one that proactively seeks to grow and is not constrained by the resources currently under its control.

Contemporary Perspectives

While these perspectives suggest an evolution of thought regarding entrepreneurship, elements of all of them can be found in contemporary thinking. This assertion is based on a critical review of 77 definitions found in journal articles and leading textbooks published over a five-year period. We performed a content analysis of key words on definitions appearing in journal articles from *Entrepreneurship: Theory and Practice*, the *Journal of Business Venturing*, the *Journal of Small Business Management*, and the *American Journal of Small Business*, as well as textbooks from major publishing houses that have achieved widespread adoption.

The results are summarized in Table 2.2. As can be seen, fifteen key terms appear at least five times in the sample. The most common terms include starting or creating a new venture; innovating or creating new combinations of resources; pursuing opportunity; the marshaling of necessary resources; risk-taking; profit-seeking; and creating value. These findings are consistent with the results of a delphi study by Gartner (1990), in which he surveyed 36 scholars and 8 business leaders. Based on a set of 90 attributes, Gartner found the greatest emphasis was placed on creating a new venture, adding value, capitalizing on opportunity, bringing resources to bear, and implementing innovations.

Synthesizing the Different Perspectives

Gartner (1990) concludes that a universal definition has yet to emerge but suggests we are talking about a single phenomenon. It is, further, a phenomenon with multiple components. The relative importance of these different components can differ based on the environmental context within which an entrepreneurial event occurs.

And yet, it would seem that the available perspectives can be synthesized into a unified framework. First, the focus should be on the process rather than the (entrepreneurial) person, while recognizing the indispensable role played by the person. Second, it is helpful to distinguish components that are inputs during the entrepreneurial process from those that are outcomes. For instance, the entrepreneurial person represents an input, while economic growth is an outcome. Third, it should be recognized that the set of necessary inputs is fairly definite, while the set of possible outcomes may or may not happen.

Accordingly, the following is proposed as a synthesis of contemporary thought:

 Entrepreneurship is the process through which individuals and teams create value by bringing together unique packages of resource inputs to exploit opportunities in the environment. It can occur in any organizational context and results in a variety of possible outcomes, including new ventures, products, services, processes, markets, and technologies.

Table 2.2
Key Terms Identified in Content Analysis of 75 Contemporary Definitions of Entrepreneurship*

		# of Mentions
1.	Starting/founding/creating	41
2.	New business/new venture	40
3.	Innovation/new products/new market	39
4.	Pursuit of opportunity	31
5.	Risk-taking/risk management/uncertainty	25
6.	Profit-seeking/personal benefit	25
7.	New combinations of resources, means of production	22
8.	Management	22
9.	Marshalling resources	18
10.	Value creation	13
11.	Pursuit of growth	12
12.	A process activity	12
13.	Existing enterprise	12
14.	Initiative-taking/getting things done/proactiveness	12
15.	Create change	9
16.	Ownership	9
17.	Responsibility/source of authority	8
18.	Strategy formulation	6

*Terms receiving five or more mentions.

THE VARIABLE NATURE OF ENTREPRENEURSHIP

Entrepreneurship has attitudinal and behavioral components. Attitudinally, it refers to the willingness of an individual or organization to embrace new opportunities and take responsibility for effecting creative change. This willingness is sometimes referred to as an ''entrepreneurial orientation.'' Behaviorally, it includes the set of activities required to move a concept or idea through the key stages in the entrepreneurial process to implementation.

Underlying entrepreneurial attitudes and behaviors are three key dimensions:

innovativeness, risk-taking, and proactiveness (Covin and Slevin, 1989; Miller, 1983; Morris and Sexton, 1996). These dimensions are illustrated in Figure 2.1 and will be explored in further detail in Chapter Four. Innovativeness refers to the seeking of creative, unusual, or novel solutions to problems and needs. These solutions take the form of new technologies and processes, as well as new products and services. Risk-taking involves the willingness to commit significant resources to opportunities having a reasonable chance of failure. These risks are typically moderate and calculated. Proactiveness is concerned with implementation, with doing whatever is necessary to bring an entrepreneurial concept to fruition. It usually involves considerable perseverance, adaptability, and a willingness to assume some responsibility for failure.

To the extent that an undertaking demonstrates some amount of innovativeness, it can be considered an entrepreneurial event and the person behind it an entrepreneur. Further, any number of entrepreneurial events can be produced in a given time period. Accordingly, entrepreneurship is not an either-or determination but a question of "how often" and "how much."

The variable nature of entrepreneurship is illustrated in Figure 2.2. The vertical axis represents the "how often" aspect or the *frequency* of entrepreneurship (number of entrepreneurial events), while the horizontal axis captures the "how much" dimension or the *degree* of entrepreneurship (the extent to which such events are innovative, risky, and proactive). Further, as illustrated in the model, the concept of *entrepreneurial intensity* (EI) is introduced to capture the combined effects of both the frequency and degree of entrepreneurial behaviors. Importantly, this framework describes the phenomenon of entrepreneurship at both the micro (i.e., the individual entrepreneur or organization) and the macro (i.e., the national or global region) levels. In later chapters, we shall elaborate on this concept and its application on various levels.

AN INTEGRATIVE MODEL OF ENTREPRENEURSHIP

Now let us try to bring all of these ideas together to provide an integrative model regarding the nature of entrepreneurship. Figure 2.3 illustrates such a model. The input-output approach to the definition of entrepreneurship has been expounded upon to include the process perspective and to incorporate the variable nature of entrepreneurship (i.e., intensity). Moreover, the proposed model

Figure 2.1
Underlying Dimensions of Entrepreneurship

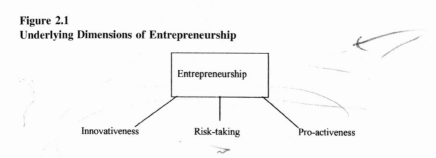

Figure 2.2
The Variable Nature of Entrepreneurship

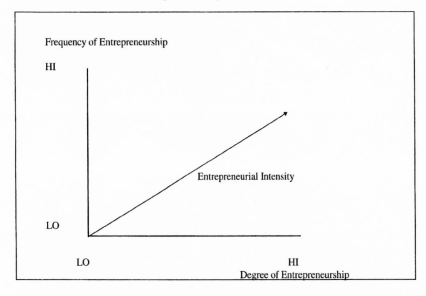

Figure 2.3
An Integrative Model of Entrepreneurial Inputs and Outcomes

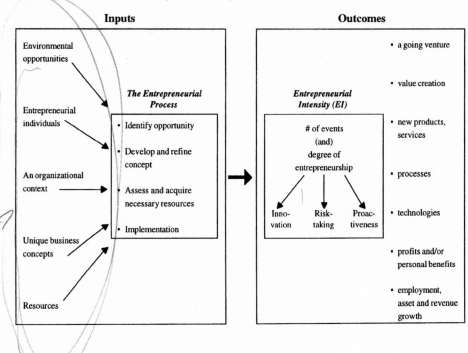

reflects the arguments in the literature regarding the importance of innovation and growth orientation by acknowledging that both are possible outcomes of the entrepreneurial process.

The input component of Figure 2.3 focuses on the entrepreneurial process itself and identifies five key elements that contribute to that process. The first is environmental opportunities, such as a demographic change, the development of a new technology, or a modification to current regulations. Next is the individual entrepreneur, the person who assumes personal responsibility for conceptualizing and implementing a new venture. The entrepreneur develops some type of business concept to capitalize on the opportunity (e.g., a creative approach to solving a particular customer need). Implementing this business concept typically requires some type of organizational context, which could range from a sole proprietorship run out of the entrepreneur's home, or a franchise of some national chain, to an autonomous business unit within a large corporation. Finally, a wide variety of financial and non-financial resources are required on an ongoing basis. These key elements are then combined over the stages of the entrepreneurial process. Stated differently, the process provides a logical framework for organizing entrepreneurial inputs.

The output component of Figure 2.3 first includes EI. Thus, the process can result in any number of entrepreneurial events and can produce events that vary considerably in terms of how entrepreneurial they are. Based on this level of intensity, final outcomes can include one or more going ventures, value creation, new products and processes, profit, and economic growth. Moreover, the final outcome is often failure, and the economic, psychic, and social costs associated with failure.

The model not only provides a fairly comprehensive picture regarding the nature of entrepreneurship, it can also be applied at different levels. For example, at the organizational level, the model describes the phenomenon of entrepreneurship in both the independent start-up company and the venture that is developed within a strategic business unit of a large corporation. Similarly, the input-output perspective is descriptive of entrepreneurship in not-for-profit organizations, with the outputs taking on slightly different interpretations, such as the creation of social value or growth measured in number of volunteers or dollars of contributions.

It is also possible to examine the input-output framework at the societal level. Much like organizations, countries would appear to differ in terms of their EI (e.g., Hughes, 1986; Wilken, 1979). These differences can be traced to the relative availability of the inputs described in Figure 2.3. Moreover, outputs such as the overall rate of new product introduction, national value added, economic growth rates, and societal wealth appear to be related to the relative emphasis on the entrepreneurial process within a society (Birch, 1981; Morris and Lewis, 1991).

CONCLUSIONS

In this chapter, we have attempted to clarify the nature of entrepreneurship by adopting an input-output perspective. The input component enables us to focus on the process nature of entrepreneurship and distinguishes the entrepreneur from the entrepreneurial process. The output component stresses the variable nature of entrepreneurship and recognizes the variety of possible consequences that can result when the inputs are combined.

Arguably, the inputs cited in Figure 2.1 are prerequisites for successful entrepreneurship. That is, without an opportunity, or absent the key resources, the entrepreneurial process is likely to result in failure with little in the way of positive outcomes. Alternatively, even with the right set of inputs, the likelihood of any particular outcome is highly uncertain. For instance, a going concern might result, but it may not be especially profitable.

Importantly, the framework is descriptive of entrepreneurial efforts in organizations of all sizes and types. Consequently, significant implications can be drawn for both prospective entrepreneurs and practicing managers. For the entrepreneur pursuing a start-up venture, the input component of the framework is perhaps more problematic, as the organizational context must be created and critical resources are much more difficult to obtain. While the entrepreneur is able to exercise considerable latitude, he/she must be wary of overcommitting to ill-defined business concepts or pushing concepts before (or after) the strategic window of opportunity opens (or closes).

For established firms, the inputs are more readily available, since the organizational context and many of the needed resources are in place. However, the entrepreneurial individual is hard to find and keep, and the organizational environment in these firms poses numerous obstacles, such as bureaucratic structures and restrictive control systems. Managers must ensure that mechanisms exist for identifying environmental opportunities, and that there is an organizational mind-set to capitalize on such opportunities whenever possible. Further, an organizational environment that supports the activities of entrepreneurial individuals or work groups is essential for the success of the process. The culture and reward system of the enterprise must be one that encourages innovative thinking, fosters proactive behaviors, and perhaps most important, tolerates failure when appropriate. Finally, managers must be willing to allocate the resources necessary to ensure that entrepreneurial initiatives have a reasonable chance of success, despite the potential risks that must be assumed.

It is also important for entrepreneurs and managers to appreciate the varying nature of entrepreneurship. Entrepreneurial behaviors need not be revolutionary nor must they occur continuously. Rather, entrepreneurial activity can vary in accordance with the industry and environmental conditions. One might expect EI to be higher in small start-up firms, as large public corporations may be less willing to pursue ventures that effectively represent "betting the farm." Ultimately, however, managers must be sensitive to the level of EI exhibited by their firms and the appropriateness of that level in relation to the competitive environment in which they operate.

Finally, the outcomes of the entrepreneurial process will also vary across firms. While growth and profitability will typically be among the set of desired outcomes, the relative importance of each may vary significantly from firm to firm. Independent start-ups may be more concerned with cash flow and profits (which flow more directly to the entrepreneur), while established firms may focus on a variety of strategic outcomes. For instance, organizations that operate in highly volatile and rapidly changing environments may direct their entrepreneurial efforts toward achieving a competitive edge that will build the company's market share. Firms that operate in more stable or mature industries may look toward entrepreneurial initiatives to lower costs, improve efficiency, or otherwise improve organizational profitability. Under certain conditions, entrepreneurial efforts may be directed toward achieving some blend of both kinds of objectives. Regardless of the specific outcomes desired, it is important for the manager to have a clear understanding of the potential strategic benefits of the outcomes of the entrepreneurial process.

REFERENCES

Birch, D.L. 1979. *The Job Generation Process*. Washington, DC: U.S. Department of Commerce.

Birch, D.L. 1981. "Who Creates Jobs." *The Public Interest*, 65 (Fall), 62–82.

Brandt, S.C. 1986. *Entrepreneuring in Established Companies*. Homewood, IL: Irwin.

Brockhaus, R., and Horwitz, P.S. 1985. "The Psychology of the Entrepreneur." In D. Sexton and R. Smilor (eds.), *The Art and Science of Entrepreneurship*. Cambridge, MA: Ballinger Publishing, 25–48.

Carland, J.W., Hoy, F., Boulton, W.R., and Carland, J.C. 1984. "Differentiating Entrepreneurs from Small Business Owners." *Academy of Management Review*, 9, 354–359.

Covin, J.G., and Slevin, D.P. 1989. "Strategic Management of Small Firms in Hostile and Benign Environments." *Strategic Management Journal*, 10 (January), 75–87.

Gartner, W.B. 1985. "A Conceptual Framework for Describing the Phenomenon of New Venture Creation," *Academy of Mangement Review*, 10 (4), 696–706.

Gartner, W.B. 1990. "What Are We Talking About When We Talk About Entrepreneurship?" *Journal of Business Venturing*, 5, 15–28.

Hisrich, R.D., and Peters, M.P. 1992. *Entrepreneurship: Starting, Developing, and Managing a New Enterprise*, 2nd ed. Homewood, IL: Irwin.

Hornaday, J.A., and Aboud, J. 1971. "Characteristics of Successful Entrepreneurs." *Personal Psychology*, 24, 141–153.

Hughes, J. 1986. *The Vital Few: The Entrepreneur and American Economic Progress*. New York: Oxford University Press.

Kao, J.J. 1989. *Entrepreneurship, Creativity and Organization*. Englewood Cliffs, NJ: Prentice-Hall.

Low, M., and MacMillan, I. 1988. "Entrepreneurship: Past Research and Future Challenges." *Journal of Management*, 14 (2), 139–161.

Miller, D. 1983. "The Correlates of Entrepreneurship in Three Types of Firms." *Management Science*, 29 (July), 770–791.

Morris, M.H., and Lewis, P.S. 1991. "Entrepreneurship as a Significant Factor in Societal Quality of Life." *Journal of Business Research*, 13 (1) (August), 21–36.

Morris, M.H., and Paul, G.W. 1987. "Innovation in Conservative and Entrepreneurship Firms." *Journal of Business Venturing*, 2, 247–259.

Morris, M.H., and Sexton, D.L. 1996. "The Concept of Entrpreneurial Intensity: Implications for Company Performance." *Journal of Business Research*, 36 (1), 5–14.

Pinchot, G., III. 1985. *Intrapreneuring*. New York: Harper & Row.

Schumpeter, J.A. 1934. *The Theory of Economic Development*, trans. R. Opie from the 2nd German ed. (1926). Cambridge: Harvard University Press.

Sexton, D.L., and Bowman-Upton, N.B. 1991. *Entrepreneurship Creativity and Growth*. New York: MacMillan Publishing Company.

Stevenson, H.H., Roberts, M.J., and Grousbeck, D.E. 1989. *Business Ventures and the Entrepreneur*. Homewood, IL: Irwin.

Tropman, J.E., and Morningstar, G. 1989. *Entrepreneurship Systems for the 1990's*. New York: Quorum Books.

Wilken, P.H. 1979. *Entrepreneurship: A Comparative and Historical Study*. Norwood, NJ: Ablex Publishing Corporation.

3

The Process of
Entrepreneurship

INTRODUCTION

Considerable uncertainty and ambiguity surround any entrepreneurial event.
Both to the outsider and the entrepreneur, things may seem disorderly on a good
day, and chaotic on most days. By definition, the entrepreneur is attempting to
do something that has not been done before. And so, one is tempted to conclude
that entrepreneurship cannot really be managed. Innovation implies something
new, something unknown, something that has not happened yet. Management
implies control, structure, and systems. But how does one control the unknown?

The reality is that one does not. There is a real need for flexibility and adaptability in any entrepreneurial venture. Successful entrepreneurs are able to com-
bine adaptability with persistence in adjusting their concept when confronted
with the obstacles, both natural and arbitrary, that arise along the way.

At the same time, entrepreneurial events are not only easier to understand,
but they tend to achieve better results, when approached as a process. The
benefits of a process approach are many. The first, and most obvious, is that the
entrepreneurial effort can be broken down into specific stages, or steps. Although
these stages will tend to overlap, and one may have to periodically revisit an
earlier stage, they tend to evolve in a logical progression. Further, approached
as a process, entrepreneurship is not some mystical or chance event pursued
only by those who are genetically endowed to be entrepreneurs. Rather, it is a
manageable event that can be pursued by literally anyone. In addition, the entrepreneurial process can be applied in any organizational context, from the start-
up venture to the large corporation to the public enterprise. Finally, processes
are sustainable. They can be ongoing or continuous. As such, entrepreneurship
can become a normal, ongoing activity in any organization.

Numerous attempts to conceptualize the entrepreneurial process have appeared in the literature. For our purposes, we will rely and expand upon the version of the process introduced in Chapter 2 and illustrated in Figure 3.1. Here, a number of the major options that are available to the entrepreneur in each of the stages have also been identified. Let us further explore each of the stages.

IDENTIFY AN OPPORTUNITY

Entrepreneurship does not start with products (or services or other innovations). The beginning point is an opportunity, which can be defined as a favorable set of circumstances creating a need or an opening for a new business concept.

The reality is that many new concepts fail not because of the concept itself, but because there was no opportunity. An example is the so-called "better mousetrap that nobody wanted." Arguably the largest single category of new product failures, these are products that are state-of-the-art advances, ones the casual observer might find quite interesting. And yet, when the test of the marketplace is applied, not enough customers are willing to buy, either because they are already satisfied, the concept is too complex or difficult to understand, the perceived switching costs are too high, or they don't have a need.

Unfortunately, a lot of would-be entrepreneurs, both in start-up and established companies, adhere to the *Field of Dreams* philosophy. In that popular film, Kevin Costner was repeatedly told, "If you build it, they will come." All too often, new products, services, and processes are developed in isolation, where the sole focus is overcoming technical, financial, and human challenges. The market opportunity is simply assumed. The next lesson learned by many companies is that having a better product at a better price with better product availability and better customer service means nothing if the market does not exist, is too small, or is unwilling to change; if competitors are completely entrenched; or if any other components of the opportunity are inadequate.

The entrepreneur must specify exactly what the opportunity consists of and quantify its size and scope to the extent possible. What is the source of the opportunity? Is it a new market segment, a demographic change, an opening that has resulted from deregulation, or some other factor? In an attempt to systematically identify where opportunities originate, Peter Drucker (1985) proposes seven major sources:

- The unexpected—events or developments that produce successes or failures that were not expected, often because of limitations in our own assumptions, vision, knowledge, or understanding.

- An incongruity—discrepancies between what is and what "ought" to be, or between what is and what everyone assumes to be, or between efforts and expectations, or in the logic of a process.

Figure 3.1
Examples of Alternatives Available at Each Stage in the Entrepreneurial Process

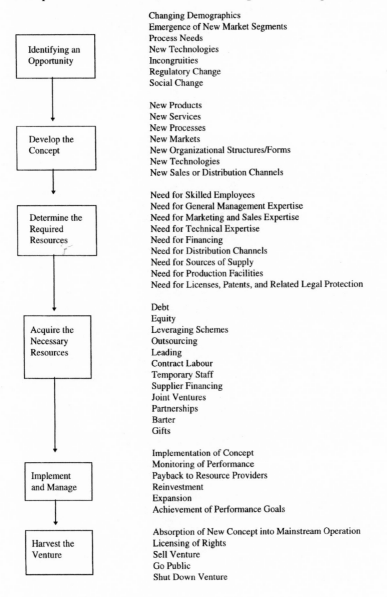

Identifying an
Opportunity

Changing Demographics
Emergence of New Market Segments
Process Needs
New Technologies
Incongruities
Regulatory Change
Social Change

Develop the
Concept

New Products
New Services
New Processes
New Markets
New Organizational Structures/Forms
New Technologies
New Sales or Distribution Channels

Determine the
Required
Resources

Need for Skilled Employees
Need for General Management Expertise
Need for Marketing and Sales Expertise
Need for Technical Expertise
Need for Financing
Need for Distribution Channels
Need for Sources of Supply
Need for Production Facilities
Need for Licenses, Patents, and Related Legal Protection

Acquire the
Necessary
Resources

Debt
Equity
Leveraging Schemes
Outsourcing
Leading
Contract Labour
Temporary Staff
Supplier Financing
Joint Ventures
Partnerships
Barter
Gifts

Implement
and Manage

Implementation of Concept
Monitoring of Performance
Payback to Resource Providers
Reinvestment
Expansion
Achievement of Performance Goals

Harvest the
Venture

Absorption of New Concept into Mainstream Operation
Licensing of Rights
Sell Venture
Go Public
Shut Down Venture

- Process needs—unmet needs or requirements within the process of a business, an industry, or a service. These needs are based on some task or job that is not currently being adequately performed or accomplished.
- Changes in industry or market structures—substantive changes in regulation, competitive entrants, power in distribution channels, technology, or market requirements that lead to industry or market restructuring.
- Demographic changes—emerging developments in the size, age, structure, composition, employment, income, or educational status of the population.
- Changes in perception, mood, or meaning—regardless of realities, general change in outlook, perception, or interpretation of the facts, which in turn influences the needs, wants, and expectations of people.
- New knowledge—development of new information, insights, technological advances, or theories.

Implicit in Drucker's analysis is the need to attack the conventional wisdom or the popular assumptions regarding a potential opportunity. Procter & Gamble's successful introduction of Depends disposable diapers represents a case in point. Introduced many years after their successful Pampers brand, which effectively created the plastic/paper diaper market for babies, Depends was targeted to senior citizens who experienced diminished bladder control or incontinence. Procter & Gamble's success was directly attributable to its defiance of the traditional assumptions that senior citizens had no money (as a group they are fairly well off), lived shut-in lives (today they tend to live active, rich lifestyles), and were too few in number (they are the fastest growing demographic segment in the United States).

A related concern is the need to recognize the existence of a "window of opportunity." For every new concept, there is an optimal time period during which it can be implemented with a reasonable chance of success. Alternatively, one can introduce something too early: for instance, before the actual number of people with a need is sufficiently large, or people are sufficiently dissatisfied with the current solution, or the necessary support infrastructure is in place. Similarly, one can introduce a concept too late: for instance, when competitors are well-entrenched, distribution channels are saturated, growth in demand has leveled off, and new technologies are emerging. In one interesting study across a number of decades, researchers found product failure was most often related to entering the market too early in the 1960's and too late in the 1980's (Bruno and Leidecker, 1988).

A good opportunity has certain characteristics. In Table 3.1, a set of criteria are presented for evaluating an opportunity, including some possible benchmarks for distinguishing attractive from unattractive opportunities. While some of these may be somewhat arbitrary, they provide some general guidelines.

DEVELOP THE CONCEPT

With an opportunity clearly in mind, the entrepreneur specifies a business concept. This could be a new product or service, a new process or method for

Table 3.1
Criteria for Evaluating Opportunities

Criterion	Stronger Opportunity ———————— Weaker Opportunity	
Market Issues		
Need	Identified	Unclear
Customers	Reachable; receptive	Unreachable or loyalties established
Payback to user/customer	Less than one year	Three years or more
Potential for value added or Created	High	Low
Likely product life	Long; beyond time to recover investment plus profit	Short; less than time to recover investment
Industry structure	Disorganized competition or emerging industry	Aggressively competitive or highly concentrated or mature industry or declining industry
Potential market size	$100 million sales	Unknown or less than $10 million sales
Market growth rate	Growing at 30% to 50% or more	Contracting or less than 10%
Gross margins	40% to 50% or more; sustainable	Less than 20%; volatile
Market share attainable (year 5)	20% or more; leader	Less than 5%
Economic/Harvest Issues		
Profits after tax	10% to 15% or more; durable	Less than 5%; fragile
Time to:		
Break even	Under 2 years	More than 3 years
Positive Cash Flow	Under 2 years	More than 3 years
ROI potential	25% or more/year; high value	Less than 15% - 20%/year; low value
Value	High strategic value	Low strategic value
Capital requirements	Low to moderate; fundable	Very high; unfundable
Exit mechanism	Present or envisioned harvest options	Undefined; illiquid investment
Competitive Advantage Issues		
Fixed and Variable Costs		
Production	Lowest	Highest
Marketing	Lowest	Highest
Distribution	Lowest	Highest
Degree of Control		
Prices	Moderate to strong	Weak
Costs	Moderate to strong	Weak
Channels of supply/ resources	Moderate to strong	Weak
Channels of distribution	Moderate to strong	Weak
Barriers to Entry		
Proprietary protection/ Regulation advantage	Have or can gain	None
Response/lead time advantage in technology; product, market innovation, people, location, resources, or capacity	Resilient and responsive; have or can gain	None
Legal, contractual advantage	Proprietary or Exclusivity	None
Sources of differentiation	Numerous, substantive, sustainable	Few or none, nominal, replicable
Competitor's mindset and Strategies	Live and let live; not self-destructive;	Defensive and strongly reactive
Other Issues		
Management team	Existing, strong, proven performance	Weak, inexperienced, lacking key skills
Contacts and networks	Well-developed; high quality; accessible	Crude; limited; inaccessible
Risk	Low	High
Fatal flaws	None	One or More

Source: Adapted from Timmons (1990). Reprinted with permission of The McGraw-Hill Companies.

accomplishing a task, or a new application of an existing product, among other possibilities. As outlined in Table 3.2, there are at least seven major categories of innovative concepts, and within the process category, ten additional subcategories.

There is a tendency to confuse the opportunity with the business concept. This mistake is one of the leading causes of product and business failure. Entrepreneurs frequently have highly innovative ideas for new product concepts, but no opportunity exists. Or, the opportunity is real, but the business concept

Table 3.2
Classifying Types of Innovations

- New to the world product or service
- New to the country and/or market product or service
- New product or service line (new to the company)
- Addition to a company's existing product or service line
- Product/service improvement, revision, including addition of new feature or option or change
- New application of existing product or service, including application to a new market segment
- Repositioning of an existing product or service
- Process improvement that leads to customer value creation, productivity enhancement, and/or cost reduction
  * new administrative system or procedure
  * new production method
  * new marketing or sales approach
  * new customer support program
  * new distribution channel or method
  * new logistical approach
  * new financing method
  * new pricing approach
  * new purchasing technique
  * new organizational form or structure

---

is too vague or unclear. Sometimes what one is calling a business concept is little more than a loosely defined opportunity, while at other times the business concept is assumed to be the opportunity.

Opportunities represent potential—potential customers, potential users, potential revenue, potential cost savings. Business concepts represent ways to capitalize on that potential with new products or services or processes. Any one opportunity could conceivably be capitalized upon with a variety of different business concepts.

Consider the social environment, and specifically, the changing nature of women's participation in the labor force. In the past 20 years, women have not only entered the workplace in larger numbers but have also tended to pursue full-time instead of part-time employment, careers instead of jobs, and senior managerial positions rather than lower-level or clerical jobs. This represents an opportunity. Successful business concepts that have capitalized on this opportunity range from L'eggs panty hose to La Petite Daycare Centers, Lean Cuisine microwaveable dinners, and Bally's Health and Racquet Clubs.

Additional examples of opportunities and related business concepts are summarized in Table 3.3. Each demonstrates the point that, while one must have a well-conceptualized business concept, success demands that the concept be clearly targeted to an untapped or inadequately tapped opportunity.

What then, is a well-conceptualized business concept? Criteria for rating a concept as good, average or weak include the need for it to be

Table 3.3
Linking the Business Concept to the Opportunity

The Opportunity	The Business Concept
Decline of demographic segmentation and emergence of youthful, lifestyle-based, market segment	Ford Mustang automobile--"affordable" sports car
Large numbers of people interested in computer possibilities but intimidated by the complexities and rigors involved in the available products	Apple personal computer with simple icons and a playful mouse
Baby boomers reaching late 30's-early 40's, with successful careers and families	Taurus automobile with state-of-art design and positioning both in terms of quality and function
Working women with active lifestyle and no time to spare	L'eggs panty hose packaged distinctively, positioned and promoted as "convenience" and distributed through grocery stores
Fast pace of change and information overload experienced by many consumers	Cable News Network (CNN) with ability to provide instant information, any time, from anywhere
Perception by many that we are generally overweight, out of shape, and/or afflicted with various health ailments	General Nutrition Centers (GNC)--national chain of health foods, vitamins, and diet products
Growing numbers of women employed full-time and/or female heads of households	La Petite Daycare Centers franchised nationally
Emergence of senior citizen market with disposable income and desire for active lifestyles	Depends disposable plastic/paper diapers
Growing need for business resources from professionals and students away from or without an office of their own	Kinko's self-help copy, computer, and communications centers

- unique
- comprehensive
- internally consistent
- feasible
- sustainable

Uniqueness refers to the need for a degree of novelty or innovativeness in a new concept. Failure commonly results from initiative, me-too new products, services, or processes, as the customer or user sees little net advantage and refuses to switch from something with which he/she is already familiar. Without sufficient uniqueness, differentiation becomes problematic. *Comprehensiveness* concerns the extent to which the new concept addresses all of the relevant strategic variables that make up the user's total value proposition. Thus, the entrepreneur must look beyond the product itself and consider such issues as packaging, pricing, distribution channels, location, and logistics. *Internal consistency* involves an assessment of how well the components above (product, location, price, distribution) work together. For instance, is the proposed distribution channel inconsistent with the target market and the product attributes being emphasized? *Feasibility* addresses the question of realism. Can the concept be developed and implemented in a timely manner and at an acceptable cost? Is our market size estimate reasonably conservative, and have we properly acknowledged the prospective customer's loyalty to, or satisfaction with, current products? Lastly, *sustainability* has to do with whether the concept, once implemented, is likely to endure in the face of competition or alternative solutions, changing costs, new technologies, or related subsequent developments. Sustainability is also a function of the entrepreneur's ability to create barriers to entry.

DETERMINE RESOURCE REQUIREMENTS

The natural tendency is to assume that the principal resource required for any entrepreneurial event is money. Money certainly matters, and entrepreneurs are notorious for over- or under-estimating their financial requirements. However, a careful review of success and failure stories makes it clear that money is only occasionally the defining factor in explaining the performance of a given entrepreneurial project. Moreover, the persistent entrepreneur with a good idea will find the money.

No, the critical resources are typically non-financial, and identifying them requires insight, judgement, and patience. For instance, creative technical skills, a loyal distributor, a permit/license or patent, well-established customer contacts, a competent manager, or a great location might prove to be determinant factors in explaining the ultimate success of a concept. The self-confidence of entrepreneurs can lead them to believe that resources such as these are secondary, or that they can do most of these things themselves. This is a recipe for failure. Entrepreneurship is about individuals who can construct, inspire, and reinforce teams, and the shrewd entrepreneur attempts to staff teams with talent to match his/her own.

ACQUIRE THE NEEDED RESOURCES

Entrepreneurship is mostly associated with the ability to come up with inventive concepts (Stage Two in the process), but the greatest amounts of entrepreneurial behavior are actually required when attempting to obtain resources and implement the concept (Stages Four and Five). Howard Stevenson (1994, p. 5) of the Harvard Business School has suggested that entrepreneurship is concerned with "the pursuit of opportunity without regard to resources currently controlled." In most cases, at the time an entrepreneur develops a concept, he/

she not only does not have the requisite resources on hand but also does not know where to get them.

Resource acquisition typically requires creative interpretation of rules. It entails begging, borrowing, and "stealing" resources from conventional and nonconventional sources. The entrepreneur in effect becomes a trader, bargainer, politician, negotiator, networker, and borrower. He/she may need to make currently owned resources appear greater than they actually are. Not surprisingly, it is in this stage that the entrepreneur also encounters a number of ethical dilemmas.

At the same time, not all resources have to be owned or directly controlled by the entrepreneur. A key concept in this regard is "leveraging." According to the dictionary, leveraging involves the mechanical advantage obtained by use of a lever, where the lever is some physical object, such as a metal rod or piece of wood. However, if we replace a few words, the concept becomes quite meaningful in a business context. Specifically, it becomes "the achievement of economic or competitive advantage through the use of resources not owned or controlled by the company."

Basically, leveraging is about renting, borrowing, leasing, chartering, contracting, or temporarily employing assets or resources instead of purchasing, employing, or owning them. It means the firm is not permanently committed to assets, which creates more flexibility and enables the firm to move more quickly in the marketplace.

Consider an example of an entrepreneur who builds a business using the leveraging concept:

* She rents her office space
* She finances the business through commercial loans
* She leases her copier, computer, company vehicle, and cell phone
* She employs only contract labor
* She outsources her production process, warehousing, accounting function, delivery service, and janitorial service
* She sells on consignment through a local retailer or through independent representatives
* She uses a plant and flower service to keep the offices looking green

And this is just a beginning. The reality is that today there are billion-dollar companies with fewer than 100 employees—everything is leveraged. Take the case of the rented or leased copier. Not only does leasing not require a large up-front capital expenditure, but copier technology is changing so fast that products are obsolete before their useful life has expired. Further, resources aren't tied up in fixed assets. Or, consider taking a loan from a bank instead of using one's own funds or attracting equity funding. The lender is the one who is tying up his/her funds, not you. Moreover, the lender is the one assuming risks for you, and the lender requires a relatively fixed return regardless of future circumstances. Finally, why would a firm choose to outsource its maintenance or information technology function? Perhaps an external vendor can do it better or cheaper because they specialize, but not always. In some cases, the firm simply determines that a certain function does not fit with its core competencies, and it can get a better return by freeing up the resources dedicated to a particular activity.

There is an even bigger benefit. Leveraging allows the firm to do more than it otherwise would. The entrepreneur can employ resources quickly and temporarily; this enables him/her to perform tasks beyond the capabilities of currently owned fixed assets and staff. It can also enhance the firm's image, while getting the staff to be more externally and opportunity focused rather than internally and resource focused.

IMPLEMENT THE CONCEPT AND MANAGE THE OPERATION

No matter how well-planned, implementation of the business concept is likely to be hectic and stressful. Tremendous learning is taking place, everyone involved in the venture is busy "doing," and the entrepreneur is faced every day with myriad decisions that must be resolved quickly. Problems and obstacles arise that were not anticipated, and a number of assumptions made when planning the concept prove to be unfounded.

Keys at this stage of the process are adaptability, tolerance of ambiguity, and a balanced internal-external focus. On the one hand, the entrepreneur must not lose sight of his/her dream or overall vision. On the other hand, he/she must be capable of adapting, modifying, and adjusting the concept, the resource requirements, the approach to acquiring resources, and the operating methods as circumstances develop. Further, given the time it takes for an entrepreneurial concept to unfold, the entrepreneur must set intermediate targets to ensure steady progress is being made along an inherently ambiguous path. In addition, the significant number of internal crises that occur, given the fact that so much learning is taking place, often creates a "fire-fighting" mentality, where the entrepreneur loses sight of external developments (e.g., with customers and suppliers).

Many entrepreneurs, brilliant as they are at putting the venture together and making things happen, are poor managers. They attempt to do too many tasks themselves and never learn to properly delegate. They tend to overcontrol employees and micro-manage the enterprise. Fear of having someone steal their innovative ideas makes them hesitant to seek advice or assistance. Further, they lead by the power of their personality. Once the venture starts to take off, they fail to bring in professional managers or institute the kinds of systems and controls necessary for sustainable growth.

HARVEST THE VENTURE

These days, opportunity windows and product life cycles are getting shorter, resources are becoming more quickly obsolete, and customer loyalties are more fleeting. Akio Morito of Sony once explained that his company's fundamental task was to make its own products obsolete. The message to the entrepreneur is not simply that he/she must be quick and nimble. Just as critical is the need for the entrepreneur to have a model regarding both how to get into the venture and how to get out.

Many possible models exist. One example might involve looking at the business as an investment in a blue chip stock versus a high-tech stock. In the blue chip stock scenario, the entrepreneur is looking for a steady, acceptable dividend each year. He/she uses the venture as a source of income into the forseeable future. With a high-tech stock, the entrepreneur expects no income as all the money is plowed back into growth and development of the business. However, he/she expects a significant capital gain in five or six years.

The model one adopts effectively defines how the concept will be harvested. One possibility is that the venture will be held onto and passed to one's heirs. Others include taking the company public, being acquired, selling the venture to a third party, licensing the rights to the concept, franchising the business, or liquidating the operation and selling off the assets.

CONCLUSIONS

In this chapter, we have explored the central notion that entrepreneurship involves a logical process. The process can be applied in literally any organizational context. The six major steps or stages in the process have been examined, and key tools and concepts for addressing each stage have been identified.

It is important to keep in mind the dynamic nature of the process. Not only do the stages overlap, but there are likely to be feedback loops between them. For instance, as an entrepreneur is developing the business concept, he/she may learn new information about the opportunity, which in turn leads to a refinement of the concept. Similarly, a change in technology or regulation may make a given resource much more affordable, which leads not only to greater reliance on that resource but also results in further modification to the concept and a change in how one plans to harvest the venture.

A related point is that opportunity tends to beget opportunity. Once an entrepreneur takes the plunge and goes after an opportunity, he/she tends to become more "opportunity aware." Moving through the stages in the entrepreneurial process is sort of like walking down a corridor, to paraphrase Ronstadt (1985). The entrepreneur suddenly becomes aware of a number of doors along the corridor that he/she never noticed before. Each door represents new or additional opportunities, and the entrepreneur, having done it once, is more likely to open some of these other doors. The danger, of course, is that everything starts to look like an opportunity, and the entrepreneur gets overcommitted or is spread too thin. Under such circumstances, one failure can bring down the entrepreneur's entire operation.

REFERENCES

Bruno, A.V., and Leidecker, J.K. 1988. "Causes of New Venture Failure 1960s vs 1980s." *Business Horizons* (November–December).

Drucker, P. 1985. *Innovation and Entrepreneurship: Practices and Principles.* New York: Harper & Row.

Ronstadt, R.C. 1985. *Entrepreneurship: Text, Cases and Notes.* Dover: Lord Publishing.

Stevenson, H., Roberts, M.J., and Grousbeck, H.I. 1994. *New Business Ventures and The Entrepeneur,* 4th ed. Burr Ridge, IL: Irwin.

Timmons, J.A. 1990. *New Venture Creation: Entrepreneurship in the 1990s.* Homewood, IL: Irwin.

4

The Concept of
Entrepreneurial Intensity

INTRODUCTION

What does it mean to say that a venture is "entrepreneurial"? As was suggested in Chapter 2, entrepreneurship is not an either-or phenomenon, it is a variable. There is some level of entrepreneurship in every person, organization, and nation. Even in the most oppressive days of communist rule in the former Soviet Union, one could find a variety of examples of people doing entrepreneurial things. Similarly, within the most bureaucratic government organizations in the United States, people such as Hyman Rickover, J. Edgar Hoover, and Robert Moses have produced significant entrepreneurship. The question then becomes one of determining how entrepreneurial a given person or event is. Again, entrepreneurship has three underlying dimensions: innovativeness, risk-taking, and proactiveness. Let us explore each of these dimensions in greater detail.

EXPLORING THE UNDERLYING DIMENSIONS OF ENTREPRENEURSHIP

Innovativeness

The first dimension that defines an entrepreneurial orientation is innovativeness. Here, the concern is with how much an entrepreneurial concept represents a departure from what is currently available. To what extent is it more (or less) novel, unique, or creative?

A range, or continuum, of possibilities exists. Does the concept address a need that has not previously been addressed, such as the first laser surgical tool? Does it change the way one goes about addressing a need, such as the fax machine or the microwave oven? Is it a dramatic improvement over conventional solutions, such as the cellular telephone or the electric automobile? Does it represent a minor modification or improvement to an existing product, such as a longer lasting lightbulb or a less fattening dessert product? Is it really just the geographic transfer of a proven product, such as the sale of frozen yogurt in a country where it is unknown?

The examples above are all products. Innovation can also take the form of new or improved services. The tremendous growth of the service sector is a testimonial to the entrepreneurial spirit at work. America Online (AOL), The Discovery Zone, and La Petite Daycare Centers represent just a few of the thousands of successful entrepreneurial service concepts. In fact, given their intangible nature and the ease with which they can be replicated, services lend themselves to continuous innovation and improvement.

The third innovation frontier is in processes, or finding new and better ways to accomplish a task or function. Many entrepreneurial ventures produce products that are fairly standard and certainly not all that unique. However, they have come up with highly innovative process innovations that are a major source of competitive advantage (i.e., they result in lower costs, faster delivery, improved quality, or better customer service). Examples include innovative production techniques, distribution approaches, selling methods, purchasing programs or administrative systems. Consider the novel hub-and-spoke transport system used by Federal Express to provide quick and dependable overnight parcel delivery service, or the highly inventive production techniques mastered by Nucor that resulted in speciality grade quality steel produced in a mini-mill.

Risk-Taking

Anything new involves risk, or some likelihood that actual results will differ from expectations. Risk-taking involves a willingness to pursue opportunities that have a reasonable likelihood of producing losses or significant performance discrepancies. Our emphasis is not on extreme, uncontrollable risks, but instead on the risks that are moderate and calculated. Entrepreneurship does not entail reckless decision making, but rather, a reasonable awareness of the risks involved—including financial, technical, market, and personal—and an attempt to manage these risks. Also referred to as "riskiness" by Venkatraman (1989), these risks are reflected in the various resource allocation decisions made by an individual or organization, as well as in the choice of products, services, and markets to be emphasized. It can thus be viewed as both an individual-level trait, as well as an organization-level construct.

An interesting perspective on calculated risk-taking is provided by Hamel and Prahalad (1993). They use the analogy of the baseball player who comes to bat concentrating hard on perfecting his swing and hitting a home run. Further, the batter is preoccupied with his batting average. Obviously, if he comes to bat only twice and gets a hit on one of those occasions, the result is a .500 batting average. Unfortunately, companies often approach the development of new products, services, and technologies as does our baseball player. They pursue few projects, rely on cautious, go-slow strategies that aim to perfect the concept, and hold off on introduction until they are certain they have a winner. Meanwhile, scrappier competitors beat them to the punch.

Successful hits are a function of both one's batting average and the number of times one comes to bat. The message is that entrepreneurs and entrepreneurial companies need to come to bat more often. Risks are better managed by focusing on frequent, lower-risk market incursions with a variety of new product and service options targeted to different segments and niches. By engaging in lots of experiments, test markets and trial runs, the entrepreneur is better able to determine what works and what does not. Such quickened learning may come at the expense of minor failures, but it is also likely to ensure more sustainable long-term success.

One might be tempted to assume that innovativeness and risk-taking are directly correlated: that doing more innovative things means taking higher risks and vice versa. In reality, the relationship may be more complex. In Figure 4.1, this relationship is pictured as a curvilinear function. As can be seen, risk is high when the company ignores new product and service opportunities, and when it pursues truly innovative opportunities. Companies that do not innovate are faced with higher risk of market and technology shifts that go unperceived and are capitalized on by competitors.

At the same time, firms that engage in breakthrough innovation are often

Figure 4.1
Relating Innovativeness to Risk

moving into uncharted waters where no one has been before. Consequently, there is high risk of market failure through improper market analysis, mismatch of technology to market needs, or inadequate design of marketing programs. In the middle of the continuum, risks are moderate, while success rates are the highest.

It is also critical to note that, from an entrepreneurial standpoint, there are actually two sides to the risk equation. Discussions of risk generally focus on what happens if the entrepreneur pursues a concept and it does not work out. This side of the equation has been labeled "sinking the boat" risk by Dickson and Giglierano (1986). It is reflected in such factors as a poorly conceptualized concept, bad timing, an already well-satisfied market, inadequate marketing and distribution approaches, and inappropriate price levels. The other side of the equation is called "missing the boat" risk, or the risk in *not* pursuing a course of action that would have proven profitable. It occurs when the entrepreneur delays acting on a concept for too long and is pre-empted by competitors or changing market requirements. Here, the entrepreneur is being too cautious or conservative and often seeks more security in the form of additional market research, financial data, or inputs from consultants.

Figure 4.2 illustrates the relationship between these two types of risk. With more planning time, sinking the boat risk steadily declines, as the entrepreneur is able to refine his/her concept, put together a better resource package, and identify more effective approaches to production, marketing and other operational concerns. Meanwhile, missing the boat risk initially falls, as the entrepreneur identifies fatal flaws that represent reasons to rethink or shelve the concept.

Figure 4.2
"Missing the Boat" and "Sinking the Boat" Risk

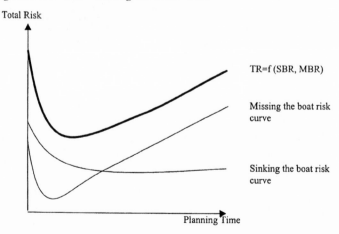

Source: Dickson and Giglierano (1986). Reprinted with permission.

He/she may let competitors be the first to the market, let them make the mistakes from which he/she can learn, then enter with a much better market solution. However, the longer the delay in action, the more likely that competitors will move quickly and lock up the market opportunity, or that the market opportunity itself will disappear. Total risk, then, becomes a function of the outcomes if one acts and if one does not.

Proactiveness

The third dimension of entrepreneurship, proactiveness, is less easy to define. The opposite of reactiveness, it is not found in the dictionary. Nonetheless, it has come into popular usage as a term to describe an action orientation. The essence of proactiveness is captured in the well-known Nike slogan "Just do it." Miller (1987) sees it as a facet of assertiveness, which he in turn views as a dimension of strategy making. He sees entrepreneurial firms as *acting on rather than reacting to* their environments. His short scale to operationalize proactiveness includes three items: following or leading competitors in innovation; favoring the tried and true versus emphasizing growth, innovation, and development; and trying to cooperate with competitors versus trying to undo them.

Proactiveness is also concerned with implementation, with taking responsibility and doing whatever is necessary to bring an entrepreneurial concept to fruition. It usually involves considerable perseverance, adaptability, and a willingness to assume some responsibility for failure. In his study of the strategic orientation of business enterprises, Venkatraman (1989) uses the term to refer to a continuous search for market opportunities and experimentation with potential responses to changing environmental trends. He suggests it is manifested and, indeed, could be operationalized in terms of

- seeking new opportunities that may or may not be related to the present line of operations;
- introduction of new products and brands ahead of competition; and
- strategically eliminating operations that are in the mature or declining stages of the life cycle.

Bateman and Crant (1993) introduce "proactive behavior" as a dispositional construct that identifies differences between people in the extent to which they take action to influence their environments. This construct holds that behavior is both internally and externally controlled, and that situations are as much a function of individuals as individuals are themselves functions of their environments. As Buss (1987) has put it, people are not "passive recipients of environmental pressures": they influence their own environments. Bateman and Crant's (1993) perspective on the essential characteristic of proactive behavior is one which fits the entrepreneurial construction very well—namely that people can intentionally and directly change their current circumstances, social or non-social.

To illustrate the proactiveness dimension, consider the engineer who works for a firm that delivers engineering services to customer sites, many of which are in remote locations. Routinely, crews must drive company trucks loaded with sensitive technical equipment to these customer sites. Traveling along bumpy, poor roads, and often dirt roads in the countryside, the equipment is often damaged or knocked out of calibration. The field crews often have to wait at a site while more equipment is sent out from the head office, or they must return another day. Our engineer takes it upon himself to fix the problem in his free time, and using resources he begs, borrows, and "steals" from the organization. Lo and behold, he comes up with a design for the truck bed that would allow the truck to be driven through a veritable hurricane, and the equipment would not come out of calibration or otherwise be damaged. Is this proactive? Yes and no. He certainly has done much more than analyze a problem; he has produced a solution. But proactiveness is more than this. He has to sell his solution to his boss, who likely will not have the time or money to support the engineer. He then has to persist in selling it to the organization, which will entail overcoming large numbers of obstacles and playing politics. If, in the end, the company's truck fleet is converted to his design, successful entrepreneurship has occurred. Even better than this would be the subsequent licensing of his design to other companies.

ENTREPRENEURIAL INTENSITY—DEGREE AND FREQUENCY OF ENTREPRENEURSHIP

The variable nature of each of these dimensions suggests that degrees of entrepreneurship are possible. Thus, a given event might be highly or nominally innovative, entail significant or limited risk, and require varying degrees of proactiveness. Further, entrepreneurship occurs in varying amounts. A given person, organization, or society might produce a steady stream of entrepreneurial events over time or generate no entrepreneurial behavior beyond the initial start-up. Organizations can be characterized, then, based on both the degree and amount of entrepreneurship they produce, or on their entrepreneurial intensity (EI).

Entrepreneurial intensity is thus a linear combination of "degree of entrepreneurship," or the extent to which events are innovative, risky, and proactive, and "amount of entrepreneurship," or the frequency with which entrepreneurial events occur. This does not mean that more of each of the three dimensions of entrepreneurship is necessarily ideal. Rather, entrepreneurship is ideally a balanced process, but the appropriate degree depends on the situation.

To visualize this, entrepreneurship might be conceived of as a vector in three-dimensional space, as shown in Figure 4.3. Three situations (E1, E2, and E3)

Figure 4.3
Entrepreneurship as a Vector

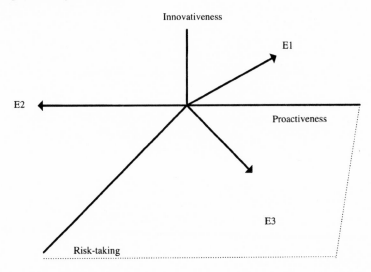

are portrayed in Figure 4.3. The first situation (E1) represents a firm, or group of managers/entrepreneurs, that is highly innovative or proactive but highly risk averse. The second situation (E2) finds another firm, or group of managers/entrepreneurs, that is highly innovative and risk-taking to the point of gambling but lacking in proactiveness—the persistence and ability to implement entrepreneurial concepts. The third firm, or group of managers/entrepreneurs (E3), has a more or less balanced entrepreneurial orientation. Two observations can be made. First, while the discussion in the figure applies to firms or groups of managers/entrepreneurs, it could just as well apply to departments or functions within firms, such as sales management or selling, and obviously the vector could be applied to an individual. Thus, there could be individuals who are indeed too innovative and not proactive enough, or who attempt to overcome personal limitations in innovativeness by taking disproportionate risks—perhaps to the extent of gambling on products, customers, or sources of supply. Second, the entrepreneurial mix, or the magnitude and direction of the vector, is obviously not standard or easy to calculate and specify. Rather, it depends on situations within industries or sales environments. Thus for example, high-tech markets might require greater levels of innovative input for success than would fast moving consumer goods markets, and real estate sales situations might reward greater risk-seeking than would situations in telemarketing.

Another worthwhile approach would be to examine the position of an organization, a department within an organization, or an individual on a matrix formed by any two of the three dimensions, and to consider the implications of this.

For example, consider a sales department within a company. The sales department might find itself in one of four positions on the risk-taking and innovativeness dimensions of entrepreneurial behavior, as illustrated in Figure 4.4. The "stuck-in-the-mud" sales manager would seldom innovate or be willing to assume the risks that such innovation would require. The "dreamer" would be highly innovative in thinking but unwilling to take risks to give the innovations a chance of success. Taking risks would be all the "wild-eyed gambler" did— the concepts on which risks were taken would not be innovative or creative but would merely be risky "bets." The entrepreneurial sales manager would balance risk-taking and innovativeness, realizing that innovative ideas also necessitate some risk-taking. Similarly, two-by-two grids can also be used to examine the dichotomies of innovativeness and proactiveness, and risk-taking and proactiveness.

THE ENTREPRENEURIAL GRID

To better understand the concept of EI, consider Figure 4.5. Here, a two-dimensional matrix has been created with the number, or frequency, of entrepreneurial events on the vertical axis, and the extent or degree to which these events are innovative, risky, and proactive on the horizontal axis. This matrix shall be referred to as the entrepreneurial grid. For purposes of illustration, five sample scenarios have been identified in Figure 4.5, and these have been labeled

Figure 4.4
Dichotomizing the Entrepreneurial Dimensions of Risk-Taking and Innovativeness

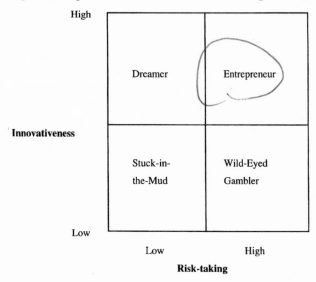

Figure 4.5
The Entrepreneurial Grid: Degree of Entrepreneurship (Innovativeness, risk-taking, proactiveness)

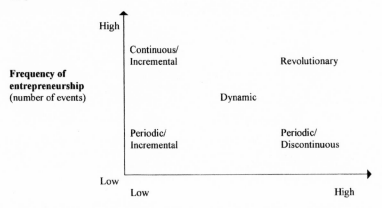

Periodic/Incremental, Continuous/Incremental, Periodic/Discontinuous, Dynamic, and Revolutionary. Each of these reflects the variable nature of entrepreneurial intensity.

For example, where few entrepreneurial events are produced, and these events are only nominally innovative, risky, and proactive, the society, organization, or individual can be described as Periodic/Incremental in terms of its (modest) level of EI. Similarly, a society, organization, or individual that is responsible for numerous entrepreneurial events that are highly innovative, risky, or proactive will fit into the Revolutionary segment of the entrepreneurship matrix and will exhibit the highest levels of EI.

While Figure 4.5 depicts five discrete segments, it is important to note that these segments have been arbitrarily defined to provide an example of how EI may vary. Amounts and degrees of entrepreneurship are relative; absolute standards do not exist. Further, any given person, organization, or nation could be highly entrepreneurial at some times and not very entrepreneurial at others. Consequently, they could occupy different segments of the matrix at different points in time.

APPLYING THE GRID AT THE LEVEL OF THE INDIVIDUAL

As noted elsewhere in this book, entrepreneurs tend to have certain characteristics in common. They are committed, determined, and opportunity-driven. They tolerate risk and ambiguity and are achievement-motivated. They tend to learn from experience. Yet, in spite of such commonalities, there is no single prototype of the entrepreneur. Some are technically-oriented, some are aggressive promoters of a concept, and others are good managers.

Some people do entrepreneurial things early in life, some do them late in life, and others do them throughout their lifetime. Similarly, the entrepreneurial events pursued by entrepreneurs will vary from being nominally innovative, risky, and proactive (e.g., the first dry cleaners to have a drive-up window, stay open twenty-four hours a day, and specialize only in cleaning men's suits) to highly innovative, risky, and proactive (e.g., Ted Turner and Cable News Network [CNN]).

Entrepreneurs can fall into different areas on the entrepreneurial grid. Figure 4.6 provides some hypothetical examples. If we consider someone like Richard DeVos, founder of Amway Products, his profile probably falls into the Continuous/Incremental segment, as his orientation has been a steady stream of complementary lines and product improvements. Bill Gates of Microsoft might be characterized as a Dynamic entrepreneur, as he has championed a substantial number of significant software innovations. Howard Head, who personally drove the development of the metal ski in the 1950's and the oversize Prince tennis racket in the 1970's, most likely falls into the Periodic/Discontinuous area of the grid. Finally, someone like Herb Kelleher, of Southwest Airlines fame, has built his very service-oriented company around a clearly defined strategy and a people-oriented management style. He probably would fall more in the Continuous/Incremental section of the grid.

Figure 4.6
Levels of Entrepreneurial Intensity among Individuals (Entrepreneurs)

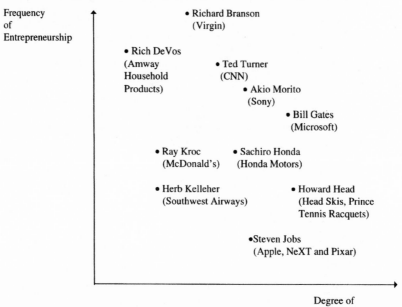

Another way in which the grid might be applied to individuals would involve characterizing how the entrepreneur approaches the external environment. Many individuals achieve success by quickly adapting to environmental change. Others base their efforts on actually creating major change in the environment. Ray Kroc was a great adapter, while Steven Jobs is more of a change agent. If we drew a vertical line at the mid-point of the horizontal, or "degree," axis, the former group would fall on the left-hand side of the grid, while the latter group would fall on the right-hand side.

Environmental circumstances are apt to influence the personal strategy one pursues in terms of where they fall in the grid. Not only might industry and market conditions influence one's personal strategy, but so too might such factors as the perceived cost of failure at different time periods, developments in one's personal life, one's past record of entrepreneurial success or failure, and the extent to which one is acting alone or in concert with others. In addition, positioning in the grid is probably influenced by other psychological traits, such as need for achievement, locus of control, risk-taking profile, and tolerance of ambiguity. The position of individuals in the grid in terms of their professional or business life is apt to differ from their entrepreneurial orientation in other domains, such as in the managment of their personal financial affairs and social relationships.

APPLYING THE GRID AT THE LEVEL OF THE ORGANIZATION

Organizations can also be characterized in terms of their entrepreneurial orientation. In fact, entrepreneurship can be an integral part of the mission, objectives, overall strategy, structure, and culture of organizations, large and small, private and public.

Consider an application of the entrepreneurial grid at the organizational level, specifically, to five successful companies (Figure 4.7). These are firms that exhibit varying degrees of EI, and as a consequence, are representative of different spaces or scenarios within the model. They include

- *Wendy's.* Started in 1969, this highly successful fast-food chain rapidly captured third place in the industry by developing an innovative product/service delivery system and by targeting a relatively untapped market consisting of young adults with a desire for higher-quality food. Throughout the years, it has maintained a competitive advantage by responding to changing environmental trends. For example, an increasing demand for convenience led Wendy's to pioneer drive-up window service, and shifting consumer preferences for lighter, low-calorie meals were met through the introduction of salads and baked potatoes. Responding to saturated demand and heightened competitive intensity, a "value menu" was added. While none of these activities can be considered highly innovative, Wendy's can be credited with introducing a few creative changes to the fast-food industry. As such, Wendy's is representative of the Periodic/Incremental segment of the entrepreneurial grid.

Figure 4.7
Entrepreneurial Grid at the Organizational Level

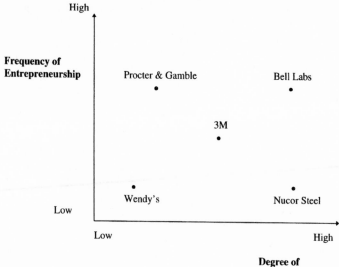

- *Procter & Gamble (P&G).* With the leading brand in 22 of the 40 product categories in which it competes, P&G has remained on top in the highly competitive consumer packaged goods industry by placing priority on research and development. The result has been a continuous stream of product improvements, with an occasional new product entry. P&G excels at evolutionary adaptations to, and improvements in, existing product concepts. Therefore, this company is representative of the Continuous/Incremental segment of the grid.

- *Nucor.* Founded in 1968 as a mini-mill that produced steel construction joints, Nucor introduced a radically new technical process for producing sheet metal in small electric arc furnaces. It mastered the ability to produce a ton of sheet steel in three-quarters of a man-hour versus the conventional three man-hours. In addition to transforming the competitive and economic structure of the steel industry, this innovation has affected the cost structure of firms in many other industries (e.g., automobile, construction). Therefore, while Nucor has been responsible for few entrepreneurial initiatives, its efforts have had a relatively dramatic effect on several industries. As such, Nucor represents Periodic/Discontinuous entrepreneurship.

- *Minnesota Mining and Manufacturing Company (3M).* 3M's unique talent is finding commercial uses for new product technology, developing that technology into dozens of marketable forms, and finding novel applications for these products. Today the firm has over 6,800 different consumer and industrial products. An example is Scotch cellophane tape, from which many successful products were derived. 3M sets a goal of achieving 25% of annual sales from products that have been developed in the last five years. The stream of innovative products that comes from this firm suggest that it is representative of the Dynamic segment of the entrepreneurial grid.

- *Bell Laboratories.* Credited with breakthrough advances in both basic and applied research, Bell Labs has earned a reputation as one of the most innovative and productive industrial research laboratories in the world. Among the labs' most notable achievements are the transistor, the laser, the solar cell, and fiber-optic transmission. The primary emphasis at Bell Labs today is developing products and processes with commercial applicability. For example, it recently developed a solution to the overcrowding of airwaves that was resulting from the increased use of cellular phones. The activities of Bell Laboratories represent the highest level of EI and, consequently, appear to fit the Revolutionary segment of the entrepreneurial grid.

These companies represent a study in contrasts. Consider a comparison of Nucor's major technological advancement in the production of steel to the constant flow of new products and processes that come from cross-functional ranks of 3M, or the development of the drive-up window concept to the development of laser technology. Yet, each firm has refined a strategy for EI that has proven to fit with its internal and external environments and to be profitable.

A company's EI score will vary depending on a number of internal and external factors. Internally, entrepreneurship is more evidenced where company structures are flat, control systems contain a measure of slack, appraisal systems include innovation and risk-taking criteria, jobs are broad in scope, and reward systems encourage a balance of individualism and group orientation. Externally, industries that are highly concentrated; and have little direct competition, demand that is captive, technologies that rarely change, and margins that are comfortable, will likely contain companies with low EI scores. Frequency of entrepreneurship may be directly related to the intensity of competition and amount of market heterogeneity, while degree of entrepreneurship is likely to be related to the rate of technological change in an industry and amount of product heterogeneity.

APPLYING THE GRID AT THE SOCIETAL LEVEL

Countries can also be described in terms of their entrepreneurial profiles. Regardless of its political, cultural, social, religious, or economic orientations, every nation produces some level of entrepreneurship. Whether measured by business start-ups, patents issued, licenses granted, significant improvements in worker productivity, or some other proxy indicator, the amount of entrepreneurship evidenced in different societies (e.g., entrepreneurship per capita) is likely to vary.

Figure 4.8 represents an attempt to categorize countries within the entrepreneurial grid. As with the applications at the individual and organizational levels, this illustration is not based on empirical evidence. Rather, it is based on subjective judgement and is only for illustrative purposes.

Figure 4.8
Entrepreneurial Grid at the Societal Level

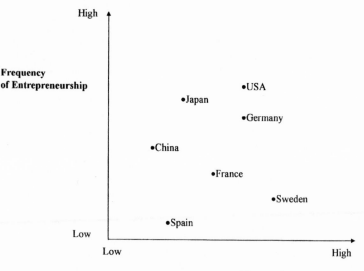

Baumol (1990) has persuasively argued that the level of entrepreneurship in a society is a direct function of society's rules (regulations and policies) governing the allocation of rewards. Further, he suggests that entrepreneurial potential is rich in every nation, but that the rules of the game determine where this potential gets channeled. In many cases, it gets channeled into unproductive or dysfunctional behaviors, such as criminal activity, speculative financial transactions that make no contribution to the productive capacity of the economy, take-overs, tax evasion, military ventures, and litigation that seeks to produce windfalls.

Entrepreneurship would also appear to be more compatible with certain countries' cultures than with others. In his landmark work on national culture, Hofstede (1980) demonstrates meaningful differences among countries on such cultural variables as individualism-collectivism, power distance, masculinity-femininity, and uncertainty avoidance. He further demonstrates linkages between certain of these variables and other variables (e.g. Confucianism, dynamism) and national wealth and economic growth.

Other findings demonstrating relationships between entrepreneurial activity, on the one hand, and both national wealth and economic growth, on the other, would suggest that certain cultural values and norms directly conflict with innovative, risk-taking, proactive behaviors.

MEASURING ENTREPRENEURIAL INTENSITY

The discussion up to this point has implied that EI can be measured. While reliable and valid measures have yet to be developed at the individual and societal levels, progress has been made at the organizational level. Building on the work of Miller and Friesen (1983), a number of researchers have reported success both in measuring a company's entrepreneurial orientation and in linking that orientation to various strategic and performance variables.

One adaptation of these measures is presented in Table 4.1. The items in this questionnaire capture both the degree and frequency of entrepreneurship, as well as the underlying dimensions of innovativeness, risk-taking, and proactiveness. In addition, both product or service and process innovation are covered. Various studies in which these measures have been employed have reported more than satisfactory statistics for their reliability and validity.

Using measures such as those in Table 4.1, researchers have demonstrated statistically significant relationships between EI and a number of indicators of company performance. Examples of such indicators include profits, the income-to-sales ratio, the rate of growth in revenue, the rate of growth in assets, the rate of growth in employment, and a composite measure of twelve financial and non-financial criteria (Covin and Slevin, 1989, 1990; Davis, Morris and Allen, 1991; Miller and Friesen, 1983; Morris and Sexton, 1996; Peters and Waterman, 1982; Zahra, 1986). This linkage between EI and performance appears to be especially strong for companies that operate in increasingly turbulent environments.

The measurement of EI also provides numerous opportunities for further research. For example, the relative importance of degree and frequency when measuring EI may actually vary depending on certain strategic factors, such as the pace of technological change in an industry, the levels of competitive intensity, or the heterogeneity of market demand. Research is needed to identify the conditions under which degree or frequency is the strongest contributor to performance. It is also necessary to determine if frequency and degree contribute equally to short-term as opposed to long-term performance. It may be that frequency has more of a short-term impact, whereas degree is better able to impact long-term outcomes. Although hypothetical, such a possibility is implicit in the work of Hamel and Prahalad (1991). Using a baseball analogy of hitting many singles versus attempting to hit a home run, they emphasize the value of companies pursuing multiple smaller projects at a time as opposed to pursuing a potentially breakthrough project. A risk-reward trade-off is involved in which the former are thought to generate short- and intermediate-term profits, whereas the latter significantly impact long-term profitability.

Research might also be directed toward identifying realistic time lags between a decrease or increase in EI within a firm and changes in organizational performance. This would require the development of longitudinal databases. The lag may vary depending on where the organization finds itself on the EI con-

Table 4.1

The Entrepreneurial Performance Index (applied to South African companies)

I. New Product Introduction

1. What is the number of new products your company introduced during the past two years? _____

	Significantly less		Same	Significantly more	
2. How does the number of new product introductions your company made compare with those of your major competitors?	1	2	3	4	5
3. To what degree did these new product introductions include products that had not previously existed anywhere before ("new to the world")?	1	2	3	4	5
4. To what degree did these new product introductions include products that did not previously exist in your markets ("new to the South African market")?	1	2	3	4	5
5. To what degree did these new product introductions represent modifications to current products or extensions of current product lines?	1	2	3	4	5

II. New Service Introduction

1. What is the number of new services your company introduced during the past two years? _____

	Significantly less		Same	Significantly more	
2. How does the number of new service introductions your company made compare with those of your major competitors?	1	2	3	4	5

	Not at all			To a great extent	
3. To what degree did these new service introductions include services that had not previously existed anywhere before ("new to the world")?	1	2	3	4	5
4. To what degree did these new service introductions include services that did not previously exist in your markets ("new to the South African market")?	1	2	3	4	5
5. To what degree did these new service introductions represent modifications to current services or an extension of your current service line?	1	2	3	4	5

Table 4.1 (continued)

III. New Process Introduction

1. Please estimate the number of new production or operational processes your company implemented during the past two years. Examples of process innovations include: new systems for managing inventories, an improved process for collecting unpaid accounts, major new sales or distribution approaches, etc. ————

	Significantly less		Same		Significantly more
2. How does the number of new production or operational process introductions your company made compare with those of your major competitors?	1	2	3	4	5
	Minor				Major
3. To what extent did these new process improvements represent a minor or major modification of existing processes?	1	2	3	4	5

IV. Company Orientation

For the following statements, please circle a number that best corresponds to your level of agreement with each statement.

Our company is characterized by:	Strongly agree				Strongly disagree
1. a high rate of new product/service introduction, compared to our competitors (including new features and improvements);	1	2	3	4	5
2. an emphasis on continuous improvement in methods of production and/or service delivery;	1	2	3	4	5
3. risk-taking by key executives in seizing and exploring chancy growth opportunities;	1	2	3	4	5
4. a "live and let live" philosophy in dealing with competitors;	1	2	3	4	5
5. seeking of unusual, novel solutions by senior executives to problems via the use of "idea people," brainstorming, etc.;	1	2	3	4	5
6. a top management philosophy that emphasizes proven products and services, and the avoidance of heavy new product development costs;	1	2	3	4	5
7. a charismatic leader at the top.	1	2	3	4	5
At our company, top level decision making is characterized by:	Strongly agree				Strongly disagree
8. cautious, pragmatic, step-at-a-time adjustments to problems;	1	2	3	4	5

Table 4.1 (continued)

9. active searches for big opportunities;	1	2	3	4	5
10. rapid growth as the dominant goal;	1	2	3	4	5
11. large, bold decisions despite uncertainties of the outcomes;	1	2	3	4	5
12. compromises among the conflicting demands of owners, government, management, customers, employees, suppliers, etc.;	1	2	3	4	5
13. steady growth and stability as primary concerns.	1	2	3	4	5

V. Key Business Behavioral Dimensions

The following questions relate to the situational factors that face individuals in your organization on a day-to-day basis. Please circle the number that best represents the emphasis your company places on the two criteria given. The number 1 means more emphasis is placed on the left and number 5 more emphasis on the right.

1. When it comes to our company's current strategic orientation, we are:

Influenced primarily by the resources we currently control.	1	2	3	4	5	Influenced primarily by the perception of untapped opportunity.

2. When it comes to our company's approach to new opportunities, we tend to:

Commit fairly quickly, capitalize and move to the next opportunity.	1	2	3	4	5	Approach with an evolutionary commitment that tends to be of long duration,

3. Our company's approach to investing resources in new opportunities tends to involve:

Multiple stages with minimal commitment at each stage.	1	2	3	4	5	A single stage with complete commitment upon decision.

4. When it comes to the way in which we manage or control resources, we prefer:

Episodic use, renting, leasing, contracting, and outsourcing of resources.	1	2	3	4	5	Ownership, purchase, control, and employment of the resources we use.

5. Our company's management structure can be characterized as:

A flat structure with multiple informal networks.	1	2	3	4	5	A hierarchical structure with clearly defined authority and responsibility.

6. Our company's compensation and reward system is:

Value based and team based with unlimited earnings potential for employees.	1	2	3	4	5	Resource based, driven by short-term performance data, with limited earning potential for employees.

tinuum, as well as on the relative emphasis placed on the degree versus the frequency components of EI.

Research should also be directed toward establishing the types and amounts of costs associated with EI. Resource requirements are likely to vary considerably at different levels of EI within a given industry, and the shape of the cost curve should be estimated. A related question concerns the failures that result from EI. Product and service failure rates are likely to be positively associated with both the frequency and degree components of EI, and research is needed to determine which is greater and why.

Another fertile area for researchers involves the role of EI in determining environment-strategy-structure relationships. It would seem that EI serves a potentially critical role in integrating these three variables. As a case in point, firms experiencing higher levels of environmental turbulence may require higher levels of EI to survive and grow, which in turn generates corporate strategies that are more aggressive (e.g., prospecting, acquisition) as well as structures that are more flexible, decentralized, and open.

Finally, the robustness of the EI concept and the EI measures presented here must be established. Whereas a wide variety of organizational contexts should be explored, it might be especially worthwhile to examine the application of EI to non-profit and government organizations. Progress in these areas is likely to require additional work in defining what constitutes a new product, service, or process and in establishing the strategically meaningful measures of performance.

CONCLUSIONS

There is a growing research foundation to support the concept of EI. Keats and Bracker (1988) use the term in characterizing different types of entrepreneurs and suggest that organizational performance is affected by intensity. Stuart and Abetti (1987), in a study of factors contributing to venture success, examined a variable they termed "organic emphasis" to describe the extent to which a firm's internal environment and culture are innovative, opportunistic, and risk-taking, as well as a variable labeled "entrepreneurship level" to reflect the degree to which a firm's leaders demonstrated characteristics associated with the entrepreneurial personality. Schaefer (1990) assesses "levels of entrepreneurship" in an organizational context. Jennings and Seaman (1990) discuss the "entrepreneurial aggressiveness" of savings and loan institutions, as reflected behaviorally in their financial portfolios. Cheah (1990) proposes a continuum of entrepreneurial possibilities based on the extent to which the entrepreneur is creating significant new profit opportunities (disturbing the equilibrium) versus capitalizing on available opportunities (bringing disequilibrium into equilibrium). Covin and Slevin (1991) refer to the "entrepreneurial posture" of firms.

Although both frequency and degree are implicit in much of the available research, the distinction between the two has not been sufficiently emphasized.

For instance, Cheah's conceptual argument appears to emphasize degree, whereas the measures used by Jennings and Seaman seem to focus more on frequency. Alternatively, Covin and Slevin mention the "extensiveness and frequency of product innovation," and Schaeffer examines how entrepreneurial decision making is in general, as well as the number of new services introduced by the firms she studied.

This distinction is clearly delineated in the entrepreneurial grid and the sample measures presented in this chapter. A central thesis of this book is that EI should be used as a key activity ratio that is monitored and measured on an ongoing basis. Measurement at the level of the individual can be useful in helping managers and others to examine and refine their own leadership styles, as well as in characterizing employee behavior over time. At the organizational level, measures can be used to benchmark and track entrepreneurial performance, establish norms and draw industry comparisons, establish entrepreneurship goals, develop strategies, and assess relationships between EI and company performance variables over time. Societal measurement of EI can be valuable in benchmarking and making cross-national comparisons. Measures of EI can be correlated with national wealth, economic growth rates, and various measures of societal quality-of-life dimensions. Such measures also represent a focal point of public policy effort, as public officials attempt to establish "rules of the game" that determine the relative emphasis on the frequency versus degree of entrepreneurial effort in society.

REFERENCES

Bateman, T.S., and Crant, J.M. 1993. "The Proactive Component of Organizational Behavior: A Measure and Correlates." *Journal of Organizational Behavior*, 14 (March), 103–118.

Baumol, W.J. 1990. "Entrepreneurship: Productive, Unproductive, and Destructive." *Journal of Political Economy*, 98 (5), 893–921.

Buss, D.M. 1987. "Selection, Evocation and Manipulation." *Journal of Personality and Social Psychology*, 53 (4), 1214–1221.

Cheah, H.B. 1990. "Schumpeterian and Austrian Entrepreneurship: Unity within Duality." *Journal of Business Venturing*, 5 (December), 341–347.

Covin, J.G., and Slevin, D.P. 1989. "Strategic Management of Small Firms in Hostile and Benign Environments." *Strategic Management Journal*, 10 (1), 75–87.

Covin, J.G., and Slevin, D.P. 1991. "A Conceptual Model of Entrepreneurship as Firm Behavior." *Entrepreneurship Theory and Practice*, 16 (Fall), 7–25.

Davis, D., Morris, M., and Allen, J. 1991. "Perceived Environmental Turbulence and Its Effect on Selected Entrepreneurship, Marketing and Organizational Characteristics in Industrial Firms." *Journal of the Academy of Marketing Science*, 19 (Spring), 43–51.

Dickson, P.R., and Giglierano, J.J. 1986. "Missing the Boat and Sinking the Boat: A Conceptual Model of Entrepreneurial Risk." *Journal of Marketing*, 50, 43–51.

Hamel, G., and Prahalad, C.E. 1991. "Corporate Imagination and Expeditionary Marketing." *Harvard Business Review*, 69 (4) (July–August), 31–93.

Hofstede, G. 1980. "Motivation, Leadership and Organization: Do American Theories Apply Abroad?" *Organizational Dynamics*, 9 (3), 42–63.

Jennings, D.F., and Seaman, S.L. 1990. "Aggressiveness of Response to New Business Opportunities Following Deregulation: An Empirical Study of Established Financial Firms." *Journal of Business Venturing*, 5 (October), 177–189.

Keats, B.W., and Bracker, J.S. 1988. "Toward a Theory of Small Business Performance: A Conceptual Model." *American Journal of Small Business*, 13 (Spring), 14–58.

Miller, D., and Friesen, P.H. 1983. "Innovation in Conservative and Entrepreneurial Firms: Two Models of Strategic Momentum." *Strategic Management Journal*, 3 (1), 1–25.

Miller, D. 1987. "Strategy Making and Structure: Analysis and Implications for Performance." *Academy of Management Journal*, 30 (1), 7–32.

Morris, M.H., Sexton, D., and Lewis, P. 1994. "Reconceptualizing Entrepreneurship: An Input-Output Perspective." *SAM Advanced Management Journal*, 59 (1) (Winter), 21–31.

Morris, M.H., and Sexton, D.L. 1996. "The Concept of Entrepreneurial Intensity." *Journal of Business Research*, 36 (1), 5–14.

Peters, T., and Waterman, R. 1982. *In Search of Excellence.* New York: Harper & Row.

Schaefer, D.S. 1990. "Level of Entrepreneurship and Scanning Source Usage in Very Small Businesses." *Entrepreneurship Theory and Practice*, 15 (1), 19–31.

Stuart, R., and Abetti, P.A. 1989. "Start-up Ventures: Towards the Prediction of Initial Success." *Journal of Business Venturing*, 2 (3), 215–230.

Venkatraman, N. 1989. "Strategic Orientation of Business Enterprises: The Construct, Dimensionality, and Measurement." *Management Science*, 35 (August), 942–962.

Zahra, S.A. 1986. "A Canonical Analysis of Corporate Entrepreneurship Antecedents and Impact on Performance." In *Best Paper Proceedings*, Pearce and Robinson (eds.), 46th Annual Meeting, Academy of Management, 71–75.

5

The Environment for Entrepreneurship

INTRODUCTION

Based on the discussion in Chapter 4, the level of entrepreneurial intensity (EI) can be expected to vary considerably among persons, companies, industries, geographic regions, and nations. In the United States, for instance, entrepreneurial efforts resulted in sizeable contributions to the gross national product and the standard of living in the second halves of the nineteenth and the twentieth centuries. But such efforts were much less significant in Mexico during the same period.

The question is, Why? Americans are not inherently any more entrepreneurial than are Mexicans. Nor are people in Taiwan inherently more entrepreneurial than those in China, although there are probably differences between the two in what Davidsson (1992) calls their "entrepreneurial culture scores," a measure of mental preparedness and drive to exhibit entrepreneurial behavior. In the same vein, there must be some logical reason why immigrant populations produce more entrepreneurship per capita than non-immigrant populations, and why some think that first-born children pursue an entrepreneurial path more often than second- or third-born children.

Such situational differences can be traced to the context within which entrepreneurship occurs. It is important that we dispense once and for all with the notion that entrepreneurship is a function of genetics, luck, cyclical patterns, uncontrollable circumstances, or just being in the right place at the right time. Entrepreneurship is neither innate to certain people and societies nor a random or chance event. Rather, it is determined by environmental conditions operating at a number of levels.

There are, of course, hundreds of variables operating in a given environment that could inhibit or facilitate entrepreneurial behavior. In Figure 5.1, we attempt to capture these environmental variables by grouping them into three general categories. These include

- the environmental infrastructure which characterizes a society;
- the degree of environmental turbulence present in a society; and
- the personal life experiences of a society's members.

The combined effect of these three environmental influences is the level of EI in a society. Although these environmental influences are admittedly inter-dependent, each represents a relatively distinct construct that has a differential impact on societal entrepreneurship. Let us examine all three in more detail.

ENVIRONMENTAL INFRASTRUCTURE

We use the term "environmental infrastructure" loosely to capture the eco-nomic, political, legal, financial, logistical, educational, and social structures that characterize a society. As proposed in Figure 5.2, certain structures would appear to facilitate entrepreneurial attitudes and behaviors. For instance, in places like

Figure 5.1
A Model of the Environmental Determinants of Entrepreneurship

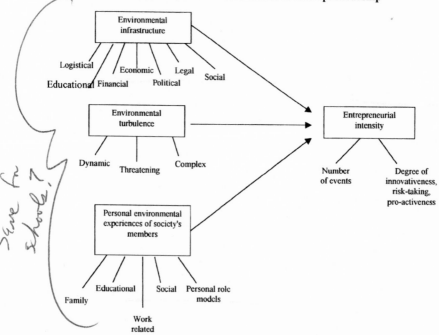

Figure 5.2
Infrastructure and Entrepreneurship

Hong Kong that have had relatively free, competitive market economies, available pools of capital, limited regulation, and political freedom, entrepreneurship is more in evidence.

Certain aspects of the economic system can act as incentives for individuals and help ensure that scarce economic resources are allocated to value-creating activities. They include freely fluctuating prices, private ownership, strong profit incentives, limited taxation, and a limited role for government. Governments can play a role in ensuring that these market mechanisms function more efficiently by removing conditions that create entry barriers, market imperfections, and administrative rigidities. Economic policies that encourage low levels of inflation without excessive interest rates also play a role.

Similarly, a political system fosters entrepreneurship when it is built around freedom of choice, individual rights, democratic rule, and a series of checks and balances among the executive, legislative, and judicial branches of government (Friedman, 1982; Schumpeter, 1950). Such designs are apt to be more accepting of innovation in all walks of life. Further, policy initiatives that facilitate or incentivize entrepreneurial activity (e.g., incubator programs, tax incentives) play a meaningful role in reinforcing an entrepreneurial ethic (Willis, 1985).

Legal and regulatory structures are significant positive factors to the extent that they recognize the corporate form of enterprise, permit limited liability, ensure contract enforcement and intellectual property protection, allow liberal treatment of bankruptcy, encourage competition, and impose fairly strong restrictions on monopolistic (restraint of trade) practices. These encourage risk-taking and pre-empt many of the obstacles to new product and process development. Alternatively, entrepreneurs are clearly discouraged from starting ventures where they are forced to comply with many rules and procedural requirements, must report to an array of institutions, and have to spend extensive time and money in fulfilling the documentation requirements. The evidence also suggests that regions with corrupt governments, and a concentration of parastatals or government-run industries, find the development of new ventures with growth potential to be highly problematic.

Financial systems are more encouraging of entrepreneurship when they are developed around institutional autonomy, competition among sources of capital, competitive interest rates, stable currencies, partial reserve requirements, well-backed deposit insurance, and large private investment pools (Birch, 1981; Brophy, 1982; Kent, 1986). These characteristics give rise to more diverse investment strategies by the mainstream financial institutions, novel types of investment organizations, and creative financing mechanisms. Further, research has shown that the establishment rates for new businesses are associated with the creation of investment companies, provision of low interest loans, and availability of credit guarantee schemes. As a result, individuals and organizations wishing to engage in entrepreneurial activity find the supply of financial resources is greater, and there are more choices in the trade-offs that must be made to obtain funding (Brophy, 1982; Eisenhardt and Forbes, 1984).

This is important, given that entrepreneurs require financial assistance for at least one of three different purposes: to diversify or spread start-up risk, to generate start-up capital, and to finance growth and expansion. Moreover, traditional bankers tend to lack both the inclination and the expertise necessary to support a wide range of entrepreneurial activity (Vesper, 1994).

Educational structures also play a role. Low levels of technical and business skills are a major deterrent to the starting of new ventures (Vesper, 1990; Davidsson, 1991). In addition, the skills and knowledge required for entrepreneurial success tend to vary across the different stages of business development. It is also noteworthy that evidence from the developed economies suggests that the educational background of start-up entrepreneurs has increased substantially in recent decades. Both government-sponsored and private training courses can positively impact entrepreneurship (Management Systems International, 1990). Other evidence suggests the presence of colleges and universities for training and research is an important facilitator. In one noteworthy U.S. study, Phillips (1993) demonstrated that every 1% increase in a state's college-educated population was associated with an 11.2% increase in jobs created by small firms.

Logistical arrangements include the development of roads, power grids, waterways, airports, efficient communication systems, and well-integrated channels of distribution. When these are highly developed, entrepreneurs are better able to identify and serve marketplace needs quickly and to capitalize on new methods and technologies (Aldrich, 1990; Stevenson and Sahlman, 1986). Markets themselves become more sophisticated.

Social structures that foster attitudes of individual freedom and an orientation toward self-direction and personal achievement are conducive to entrepreneurial initiatives (Birch, 1987; Tropman and Morningstar, 1989). In societies where the main concern is for the individual rather than the group, reward systems are more likely to encourage risk-taking, proactivity, and innovation. Individual goal-setting, independence, and personal ambition are recognized and encouraged in societies with individualistic social structures. Further, social systems that facilitate the development of networks to share information, identify opportunities, and marshal resources are conducive to entrepreneurial activity (Aldrich and Zimmer, 1986; Carsrud and Johnson, 1989).

Several researchers have stressed the importance of prevailing attitudes, values, beliefs and social norms—the so-called "mental software"—for explaining variations in entrepreneurship and economic development (Carsrud and Johnson, 1989; Davidsson, 1992; Etzioni, 1987; Shapero and Sokol, 1982). Alternatively, entrepreneurship will suffer if most of the members of society view it with suspicion. Both a favorable attitude on the part of society toward entrepreneurship and widespread public support for entrepreneurial activities are needed to motivate people to confront the risks, frustrations, stress, lengthy development cycles, and related hardships that are inherent in any entrepreneurial endeavor. Programs that create social awareness and social reinforcement of entrepreneurship are important. Awards programs and public recognition for entrepreneurs, news features on entrepreneurial role models, and business start-up competitions in schools are examples of vehicles that have helped create more social emphasis on entrepreneurship as a desirable path to pursue.

Further insights into ways in which entrepreneurship is impacted by the environmental infrastructure are provided by Gnyawali and Fogel (1994). In a comprehensive review, they examine empirical findings from research studies performed in a variety of countries around the world. Many of these studies are summarized below in Table 5.1.

ENVIRONMENTAL TURBULENCE

Environmental turbulence is the second component of our model. Turbulence has three components. These include the rate of change in key components of the environment, the extent to which the environment is hostile or threatening, and the degree of complexity in the environment. Turbulence in the technological, economic, customer, supplier, competitive, legal/regulatory, and social environments produces both threats and opportunities. It means the rules of the game may well be changing, and that the current assumptions may no longer hold. It suggests that certain needs no longer exist, others are changing, and new needs are appearing.

Turbulence is a major trigger, or catalyst, for entrepreneurial activity (see Figure 5.3). Consider the boom in entrepreneurial activity that occurred with the demise of the communist state in Poland. In South Africa under the former apartheid regime, the imposition of economic sanctions against the country led to extremely entrepreneurial activity as companies sought new sources of supply. The subsequent demise of apartheid has also produced a substantial increase in entrepreneurial activity. In the United States and Europe, deregulation of the telecommunications industry has produced a general lowering of prices, the ap-

Table 5.1
Selected Findings on the Role of Environmental Conditions in Facilitating
Entrepreneurship

Environmental Conditions and Research Findings	Source
Government Policies and Procedures	
In the Cayman Islands, entrepreneurship was facilitated by keeping paperwork and procedural requirements at a minimum.	Dana, 1987
In Malaysia, concentration of power in the business development agency established by the government and too many procedural requirements discouraged entrepreneurship.	Dana, 1990
In Saint Martin, excessive regulation of business suppressed growth and entrepreneurship; conversely, in Sint Maarten, minimum regulation and procedural requirements encouraged entrepreneurship.	Dana, 1990
In Mexico, key barriers to start-up included excessive government regulation, high tax rates, and increasing inflation.	Young & Welsch, 1993
Socioeconomic Conditions	
In Sweden, tax and other incentives had a greater impact on persons who were strongly motivated to start a business than on persons who were less motivated.	Davidsson, 1991
In the Czech and Slovak Republics, negative public attitudes toward entrepreneurs discouraged entrepreneurs.	Swanson and Webster, 1992
Cities having a larger number of economic development programs achieved a higher growth in the number of new firm establishments than cities having a smaller number of such programs.	Feiock, 1987
The greater the percentage of small firms in a growing sector, the greater the share of jobs created by small firms in that sector.	Phillips, 1993
Entrepreneurial and Business Skills	
In Sweden, both business-related experiences and business education were highly correlated with entrepreneurs' ability to start and manage a business.	Davidsson, 1991
In the region of Sub-Saharan Africa, entrepreneurs suffered from barriers such as the need for following societal stereotypes and traditions, a general lack of realization of the importance of thrift, and lack of perseverance.	Takyi-Asiedu, 1993
Every 1% increase in a state's college-educated population led to an 11.2% increase in jobs created by small firms.	Phillips, 1993
Financial Support	
In the Cayman Islands, creation of investment companies facilitated entrepreneurship.	Dana, 1987

Table 5.1 (continued)

Environmental Conditions and Research Findings	Source
In Singapore, provision of low-interest loans and government grants facilitated entrepreneurship development.	Dana, 1987
In the United States, availability of financial resources was an important contributor to organizational birth rate.	Pennings, 1982
In Michigan, investment by the State Pension Fund in venture capital investment attracted large venture capital companies to invest in small businesses.	Kleiman and Bygrave, 1998
In Japan, 52 credit guarantee associations exist to guarantee loans to small and medium-sized enterprises (SMEs); local governments have special funds that serve as a reserve for loans to SMEs. Consequently, most entrepreneurs got loans for start-up business.	Hawkins, 1993
In the United Kingdom, private investors are attracted to invest in new companies because the government provides tax relief for new equity investment by individuals in unquoted companies.	Harrison and Mason, 1988
In Mexico, key barriers for start-up included lack of working capital, difficulty in obtaining loans, and seasonal fluctuations in cash.	Young and Welsch, 1993

Non-Financial Support

In Australia, the provision of nationwide management training programs and the supply of textbooks and information materials on business start-up issues encouraged new business start-ups.	Dana, 1987
In the Virgin Islands, a tax concession on all businesses for 10 years, a tax concession for hotels for 20 years, and exemption from custom duty on imports of capital equipment facilitated the development of entrepreneurship.	Dana, 1987
In the Cayman Islands, a government guarantee not to tax businesses for 20 years attracted entrepreneurs.	Dana, 1987
In the United States, entrepreneurs spent nearly half of their time during business start-ups in making contacts.	Aldrich, 1986
In Japan, regional information centers gather, analyze, and disseminate technical and market information and offer free access to computers; local business development centers provide free consulting and training services; government purchases a certain quantity of the products of small enterprises every year. All of these have facilitated entrepreneurship development.	Hawkins, 1993
In Canada, the government procurement program helped firms to grow faster and to develop competence in marketing and export-related activities.	Doutriaux, 1988

65

Table 5.1 (continued)

Environmental Conditions and Research Findings	Source
In the United States, large urban areas and the presence of universities for training and research assistance were important factors contributing to the birth of new firms.	Pennings, 1982
Presence of business development assistance was significantly correlated with the share of jobs created by small firms.	Phillips, 1993

Source: Gnyawali and Fogel (1994). Reprinted with permission.

pearance of a number of new entrepreneurial firms, and many new product and service innovations.

Historically, environmental turbulence has been a factor in a large percentage of new product and technological innovations (Myers and Marquis, 1969; Wright, 1947). More recently, it has been demonstrated that the more dynamic, hostile, and heterogeneous the environment, the higher the level of innovation, risk-taking, and proactivity among the most successful firms (Covin and Slevin, 1989; Miller and Friesen, 1983). Brittain and Freeman (1980) have demonstrated that technological and demographic changes create opportunities for those positioned well to capitalize on them. Similarly, Tushman and Anderson (1986) have illustrated that technological change, whether competence-enhancing or competence-destroying, creates opportunities to be exploited through entrepreneurial behaviors.

The relatively stable, predictable business environment of the 1950's and

Figure 5.3
Environmental Turbulence and Entrepreneurship

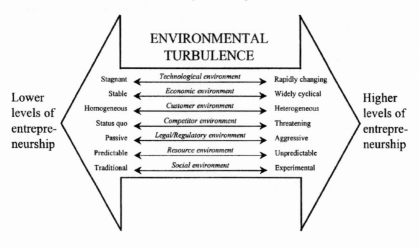

1960's led to the development of many large mechanistic organizations. Such an organizational design may be quite appropriate where customers are captive, technology rarely changes, economic conditions are favorable, and competition is passive (or the competitive rules are fixed). Static environments create less need for creative responses to changing conditions, fewer rewards for innovative behavior, and most importantly, fewer penalties for failing to innovate. But the mechanistic type of structure is inappropriate for responding effectively to dynamic, threatening, complex change. Burdened by excessive layers of management, red tape, and inflexible policies and rules, large organizations are often incapable of adapting to changes in the environment in a timely fashion. The hard lesson is that, faced with conditions where survival depends on an effective response to market variations, innovation and entrepreneurship must occur.

Today, we find ourselves experiencing historically high levels of turbulence, and environments are likely to become even more turbulent in the next few decades. As a by-product, entrepreneurs and managers are confronted with shortened decision windows, diminishing opportunity streams, changing decision constituencies, increased resource specialization, lack of predictable resource needs, fragmented markets, greater risk of resource and product obsolescence, and a general lack of long-term control. The result has been intensified pressure for innovation and a dramatic increase in societal entrepreneurship over the past two decades.

Flexible, organic structures and managerial styles are more capable of identifying potential opportunities, reallocating resources, shifting managerial commitment quickly, and developing products, services, or processes to capitalize on strategic opportunities resulting from changing conditions. Successful adaptation to environmental change requires quick, thorough, and frequent internal and external analysis, short planning horizons, and the development of flexible plans that can be adjusted as necessary. Entrepreneurial efforts and behaviors become virtually a necessity for coping with such environmental change.

These efforts, in turn, create additional environmental turbulence by bringing product and process innovations to markets and changing the way business is done (see Figure 5.4). The implication is that entrepreneurship is a response to environmental turbulence as well as a source of institutionalized societal change, where firms initiate changes in technology, marketing, or organizational design

Figure 5.4
Entrepreneurship as Result and Cause of Environmental Turbulence

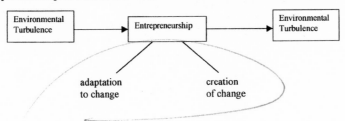

and strive to maintain the lead in changes over competitors. As the degree of entrepreneurial effort intensifies, so too does the rate of environmental change.

PERSONAL LIFE EXPERIENCES

The third and final component of our model is the personal life experiences of society's members. In addition to the influences of the infrastructure and the level of turbulence, the tendency to do entrepreneurial things is very much affected by the specific twists and turns in a given person's life.

There has been a significant amount of research into identifying the personal traits and characteristics of entrepreneurs (e.g., Collins and Moore, 1964; Brockhaus, 1980, 1982; Brockhaus and Horwitz, 1986; Birch, 1987; McClelland, 1987; Sexton and Bowman-Upton, 1990). However, attempts to develop a unique psychological profile of the entrepreneur have met with only marginal success because of the significant degree of variation among entrepreneurial types (Gartner, 1985). Most recent research has focused on the more relevant question of why the entrepreneur develops such characteristics (Delacroix and Carroll, 1983). The answer to this question is pretty clear-cut: family background, childhood experiences, exposure to role models, previous job experiences, and educational experiences all have a strong influence on the development of the entrepreneur.

Figure 5.5 is a summary of some of the types of personal life experiences thought to be associated with higher levels of entrepreneurship. Relevant aspects of family background that have been examined include parental relationships, order of birth, family income, and immigrant status. Parents instill an early sense of independence and desire for control in future entrepreneurs (Bird, 1989; Hisrich and Brush, 1984). Entrepreneurs often experience turbulent and disruptive childhoods. Particularly important is their relationship with their fathers. Several researchers have found that many entrepreneurs experienced relatively negative relationships with their fathers (e.g., Zaleznik and Kets de Vries, 1985; Silver, 1983), ranging from neglect as a result of career demands to actual physical or

Figure 5.5
Life Experiences and Entrepreneurship

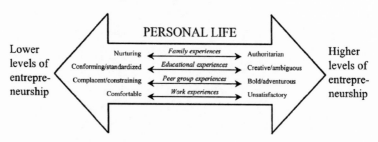

emotional abuse or abandonment. To compensate for paternal deficiencies, mothers devote themselves to helping their children succeed by instilling in them a need to excel. Having been raised with distant or uninvolved father figures, entrepreneurs develop a need for independence, self-reliance, and control. Consequently, in an effort to avoid authoritarian relationships and loss of control, and to fulfill their needs for success and achievement, individuals turn toward developing entrepreneurial ventures.

It is also argued that entrepreneurs are more often first-born children than second- or third-born, although little consensus exists on this issue. Others suggest that entrepreneurs are frequently from poorer families, and are often immigrants, or the children of immigrants (Collins and Moore, 1964; Gilder, 1984). It appears that those whose lives contain an extra degree of struggle to fit into society will more frequently develop their entrepreneurial potential.

Another important determinant of entrepreneurial behavior is the individual's exposure to successful role models (Kent, 1986; Eisenhardt and Forbes, 1984; Scherer, Adams and Wiebe, 1989; Bird, 1989; Vesper, 1990). Studies have shown that many entrepreneurs have parents who were self-employed (Hisrich and Brush, 1984; Ronstadt, 1984; Shapero and Sokol, 1982). Others find themselves working for or with an entrepreneur who becomes a role model. Another form of vicarious experience involves watching a friend develop a business. Such role models demonstrate to prospective entrepreneurs that risk-taking, tolerance for ambiguity, proactiveness, and innovation lead to independence and self-control.

Previous work experience also shapes the entrepreneur. Brockhaus (1980) found that job dissatisfaction "pushes" entrepreneurs out of established organizations and toward developing entrepreneurial ventures. In fact, the majority of entrepreneurs (59%) in Brockhaus's study indicated a desire to start their own business before they had a product or service in mind; only a small percentage (14%) were drawn away from a traditional job by the desire to market a particular product or service. Brockhaus also found that the greater the job dissatisfaction, the greater the likelihood of entrepreneurial success.

Personal experience with entrepreneurship is another factor in explaining the current or future performance of specific entrepreneurs. Whether the experience comes from ventures started on the side while in school, jobs taken on during summer breaks, or work in the family business, once a potential entrepreneur sees opportunity being capitalized upon, he/she often becomes more opportunity-aware. One of the interesting side-effects of pursuing an entrepreneurial path is the tendency to subsequently recognize additional opportunities for other ventures. Ronstadt (1984) has labeled this the "corridor principle."

Finally, educational experiences influence entrepreneurship. Some years ago, Brockhaus and Nord (1979) found that entrepreneurs had, on average, a lower level of education than managers. This tendency could lead entrepreneurs to feel limited in traditional organizations. Frustrated by an inability to achieve their desired level of success in established organizations, they choose to pursue a venture in which their own assessment of their abilities is more relevant. Some would suggest that the "school of hard knocks" prepares one better than colleges, universities, seminars, and books (Bird, 1989).

More recent evidence suggests that formal education helps entrepreneurs to succeed, and that median education levels among successful entrepreneurs have increased in the past few decades (Robinett, 1985; Ronstadt, 1985). In fact, today's entrepreneur is most likely a college graduate, and many have advanced degrees.

However, traditional teaching methods used in schools may actually stifle entrepreneurship. By stressing conformity and standardization and penalizing creative or novel approaches to problem solving, educators discourage the development of an entrepreneurial orientation in young people. Business schools and management consultants also tend to perpetuate resistance to entrepreneurship through their emphasis on structured organizational processes and decision making.

CONCLUSIONS: SPECIFYING THE PROPOSED RELATIONSHIPS

Figures 5.2, 5.3, and 5.5 each represent attempts to capture relationships between environmental variables and EI. They provide a foundation for developing clearly specified variables and formulating specific hypotheses concerning cause-and-effect relationships. Each component of the infrastructure, turbulence, and life experiences is pictured as a continuum on some characteristic. For example, political structure varies from totalitarianism to democracy, and the customer or market environment ranges from homogeneous to heterogeneous.

Two caveats should be kept in mind. First, the anchor points on each dimension are not necessarily opposites. Instead, they represent mutually exclusive alternatives that exist in varying degrees. Second, each dimension can be described in terms of a number of characteristics beyond those identified in Figures 5.2, 5.3, and 5.5. For instance, work environments could be characterized as comfortable or dissatisfactory but also as challenging, complex, stressful, or mundane. The particular characteristics cited in these figures were selected because they appear to have the most salient entrepreneurial implications.

While the relationships proposed in Figures 5.2, 5.3, and 5.5 are pictured as linear, this is not likely to be the case in actual practice. For example, financial or logistical infrastructures can discourage entrepreneurship when they are undeveloped, but also when they become overdeveloped and bureaucratic. Similarly, entrepreneurship may be fostered as environmental turbulence increases, but extreme levels of turbulence may make successful innovation impossible or remove the incentive for it.

In sum, the environmental determinants of entrepreneurship can be viewed as a set of characteristics that describe interdependent conditions of infrastructure, turbulence, and life experiences. Their effect on EI is both direct and nonlinear.

Although entrepreneurship certainly can occur under virtually any set of conditions, the relationships proposed here provide guidance for establishing conditions that foster (or suppress) the aggregate level of entrepreneurship that occurs in a given community, region, or society.

REFERENCES

Aldrich, H. 1990. "Using an Ecological Perspective to Study Organizational Founding Rates." *Entrepreneurship: Theory and Practice* (Spring), 7–24.

Aldrich, H. 1986. "Social Behavior and Entrepreneurial Networks." In R. Ronstadt, J.A. Hornaday, R. Peterson, and K.H. Vesper (eds.), *Frontiers of Entrepreneurship Research*. Wellesley, MA: Babson College, 239–40.

Aldrich, H. and Zimmer, C. 1986. "Entrepreneurship through Social Networks." In D.L. Sexton and R.W. Smilor (eds.), *The Art and Science of Entrepreneurship*. Cambridge, MA: Ballinger; 2–23.

Birch, D.L. 1987. *Job Creation in America.* New York: The Free Press.

Birch, D.L. 1981. "Who Creates Jobs?" *The Public Interest*, 65 (Fall), 62–82.

Bird, B. 1989. *Entrepreneurial Behavior.* London: Scott, Foresman and Co.

Brittain, J. and Freeman, J. 1980. "Organizational Proliferation and Density Dependent Selection." In J. Kimberly and R. Miles (eds.), *The Organizational Life Cycle*. San Francisco: Jossey-Bass, 291–338.

Brockhaus, R.H. 1982. "The Psychology of the Entrepreneur." In C. Kent, D. Sexton and K. Vesper (eds.), *Encyclopedia of Entrepreneurship*. Englewood Cliffs, NJ: Prentice-Hall.

Brockhaus, R.H. 1980. "Risk Taking Propensity of Entrepreneurs." *Academy of Management*, 23, 509–520.

Brockhaus, R.H. and Horwitz, P.S. 1986. "The Psychology of the Entrepreneur." In D.L. Sexton and R.W. Smilor (eds.), *The Art and Science of Entrepreneurship*. Cambridge, MA: Ballinger, 25–48.

Brockhaus, R.H., and Nord, W.R. 1979. "An Exploration of Factors Affecting the Entrepreneurial Decision: Personal Characteristics vs. Environmental Conditions." *Proceedings*, Annual Conference, Academy of Management.

Brophy, D.J. 1982. "Venture Capital Research." In C.A. Kent, D.L. Sexton, and K.H. Vesper (eds.), *Encyclopedia of Entrepreneurship*. Englewood Cliffs, NJ: Prentice-Hall, 165–192.

Carsrud, A.L. and Johnson, R.W. 1989. "Entrepreneurship: A Social Psychological Perspective." *Entrepreneurship and Regional Development*, 1 (1), 21–31.

Collins, O.F., and Moore, D.G. 1964. *The Enterprising Man.* East Lansing, MI: MSU Business Studies.

Covin, J.G., and Slevin, D.P. 1989. "Strategic Management of Small Firms in Hostile and Benign Environments." *Strategic Management Journal*, 10 (1), 75–87.

Dana, L.P. 1990. "Saint Martin/Sint Maarten: A Case Study of the Effects of Culture on Economic Development." *Journal of Small Business Management*, 28 (4), 91–98.

Dana, L.P. 1988. "The Spirit of Entrepreneurship and the Commonwealth Government of Australia." *Journal of Small Business Management*, 26 (1), 63–65.

Dana, L.P. 1987. "Entrepreneurship and Venture Creation—An International Comparison of Five Commonwealth Nations." In N.C. Chruchill, J.A. Hornaday, B.A. Kirchhoff, O.J. Krasner, and K. H. Vesper (eds.), *Frontiers of Entrepreneurship Research.* Wellesley: MA: Babson College, 573–583.

Davidsson, P. 1991. "Continued Entrepreneurship: Ability, Need, and Opportunity as Determinants of Small Firm Growth." *Journal of Business Venturing,* 6, 405–429.

Davidsson, P. 1992. *Entrepreneurship and Small Business Research: How Do We Get Further?* BA-Publications 126. Umeå: Umeå Business School, Sweden.

Delacroix, J., and Carroll, G. 1983. "Organizational Foundings: An Ecological Study of the Newspaper Industries of Argentina and Ireland." *Administrative Science Quarterly,* 28 (June), 274–291.

Doutriaux, J.A. 1988. "Government Procurement and Research Contracts at Start-up and Success of Canadian High-Tech Entrepreneurial Firms." In B.A. Kirchhoff, W.A. Long, W.E. McMullan, K.H. Vesper, and W.E. Wetzel (eds.), *Frontiers of Entrepreneurship Research.* Wellesley, MA: Babson College, 582–594.

Eisenhardt, K.M., and Forbes, N. 1984. "Technical Entrepreneurship: An International Perspective." *Columbia Journal of World Business,* 19 (Winter), 31–37.

Etzioni, A. 1987. "Entrepreneurship, Adaption, and Legitimation." *Journal of Economic Behavior and Organization,* 8, 175–189.

Feiock, R. 1987. "Urban Economic Development: Local Government Strategies and Their Effects." In S. Nagel (ed.), *Research in Public Policy Analysis and Management.* London: JAI Press.

Friedman, M. 1982. *Capitalism and Freedom.* Chicago, IL: University of Chicago Press.

Gartner, W.B. 1985. "A Conceptual Framework for Describing the Phenomenon of New Venture Creation." *Academy of Management Review,* 10 (4), 696–706.

Gilder, G. 1984. *The Spirit of Enterprise.* New York: Simon & Schuster.

Gnyawali, D.R., and Fogel, D.S. 1994. "Environments for Entrepreneurship Development: Key Dimensions and Research Implications." *Entrepreneurship: Theory and Practice,* 18 (4), 43–62.

Harrison, R.T., and Mason, C.M. 1988. "Risk Finance, the Equity Gap, and New Venture Formation in the United Kingdom: The Impact of the Business Expansion Scheme." In B.A. Kirchhoff, W.A. Long, W.E. McMullan, K.H. Vesper, and W.E. Wetzel (eds.), *Frontiers of Entrepreneurship Research.* Wellesley, MA: Babson College, 570–581.

Hawkins, D.L. 1993. "New Business Entrepreneurship in the Japanese Economy." *Journal of Business Venturing,* 8 (3), 137–150.

Hisrich, R.D., and Brush, C.G. 1984. "The Woman Entrepreneur: Management Skills and Business Problems." *Journal of Small Business Management,* 22, 31–37.

Kent, C.A. 1986. *The Environment for Entrepreneurship.* Lexington, MA: D.C. Heath & Company.

Kets de Vries, Manfred F.R. 1985. "The Dark Side of Entrepreneurship." *Harvard Business Review,* 63 (November–December), 160–167.

Kleiman, R.T., and Bygrave, W. 1988. "Public Sector Involvement in Venture Capital Finance: The Case of Michigan." In D.A. Kirchhoff, W.A. Long, W.E. McMullan, K.H. Vesper, and W.E. Wetzel (eds.), *Frontiers of Entrepreneurship Research.* Wellesley, MA: Babson College, 610–611.

Management Systems International. 1990. *Entrepreneurship Training and Strengthening*

Entrepreneurship Performance. Washington, DC: United States Agency for International Development.

McClelland, D.C. 1987. "Characteristics of Successful Entrepreneurs." *Journal of Creative Behavior*, 21 (2), 219–233.

Miller, D., and Friesen, P.H. 1983. "Innovation in Conservation and Entrepreneurial Firms: Two Models of Strategic Momentum." *Strategic Management Journal*, 31 (3), 1–25.

Myers, S., and Marquis, D.G. 1969. *Successful Industrial Innovation*. Washington, DC: National Science Foundation.

Pennings, J.M. 1982. "Organizational Birth Frequencies: An Empirical Investigation." *Administrative Science Quarterly*, 27 (2), 120–44.

Phillips, B. 1993. "The Growth of Small Firm Jobs by State, 1984–1988." *Business Economics*, 12 (April), 48–53.

Robinett, S. 1985. "What Schools Can Teach Entrepreneurs." *Inc.* (February), 50, 54, 58.

Ronstadt, R. 1985. "The Educated Entrepreneurs: A New Era of Entrepreneurial Education Is Beginning." *American Journal of Small Business* (Summer), 7–23.

Ronstadt, R. 1984. "Ex-entrepreneurs and the Decision to Start an Entrepreneurial Career." In J. Hornaday et al. (eds.), *Frontiers of Entrepreneurship Research*. Wellesley, MA: Babson College, 112–115.

Schumpeter, J., 1950. *Capitalism, Socialism, and Democracy*. New York: Harper & Row.

Sexton, D.L., and Bowman-Upton, N.B. 1990. "Female and Male Entrepreneurs: Psychological Characteristics and Their Role in Gender Related Discrimination." *Journal of Business Venturing*, 5 (1), 29–36.

Shapero, A., and Sokol, L. 1982. "The Social Dimensions of Entrepreneurship." In C. Kent, D.L. Sexton, and K.H. Vesper (eds.), *Encyclopedia of Entrepreneurship*. Engelwood Cliffs, NJ: Prentice-Hall, 72–90.

Scherer, R., Adams, J., and Wiebe, F. 1989. "Developing Entrepreneurial Behaviors: A Social Learning Theory Perspective." *Journal of Organizational Change Management*, 2 (3), 16–27.

Silver, A.D. 1983. *The Entrepreneurial Life*. New York: John Wiley.

Stevenson, H.H., and Sahlman, W.A. 1986. "Importance of Entrepreneurship in Economic Development." In D.C. Heath (ed.), *Entrepreneurship, Intrapreneurship and Venture Capital*. Lexington, MA: Lexington Books, 3–26.

Swanson, D., and Webster, L. 1992. *Private Sector Manufacturing in the Czech and Slovak Republic: A Survey of Firms*, Washington DC: The World Bank.

Takyi-Asiedu, S. 1993. "Some Socio-Cultural Factors Retarding Entrepreneurial Activity in Sub-Saharan Africa." *Journal of Business Venturing*, 8 (1), 91–98.

Tropman, J.E., and Morningstar, G. 1989. *Entrepreneurial Systems for the 1990s*. Westport, CT: Quorum Books.

Tushman, M., and Anderson, P. 1986. "Technological Discontinuities and Organizational Environments." *Administrative Science Quarterly*, 31, 439–465.

Vesper, K.H., 1990. *New Venture Strategies*. Englewood Cliffs, NJ: Prentice-Hall.

Vesper, K.H. 1994. *New Venture Experience*. Seattle: Vector Books.

Willis, R. 1985. "What Should Be the Federal Role in Startups?" *Management Review* (November), 11–13.

Wright, D.M., 1947. *The Economics of Disturbance*. New York: Macmillan.

Young, E.C., and Welsch, H.P. 1993. "Major Elements in Entrepreneurial Developments in Central Mexico." *Journal of Small Business Management*, 31 (3), 80–85.

Zaleznik, A., and Kets de Vries, Manfred F.R. 1985. *Power and the Corporate Mind.* Chicago: Bonus Books.

6

The Entrepreneurial Individual

INTRODUCTION

Entrepreneurship does not happen without entrepreneurs. Of all the elements necessary for successful entrepreneurship, the individual entrepreneur is the most critical. Without the visionary leadership and persistence demonstrated by this individual, little would be accomplished. As we shall discuss later in this chapter, entrepreneurship requires a team, and successful entrepreneurs tend to rely on extended networks. However, someone must come up with a concept, a vision, a dream. They must translate this dream into products and people within some sort of organizational context. They must champion the concept to a wide range of publics and partners. They must adapt the concept to reflect the realities encountered within the environment. And they must persevere in overcoming the normal and the arbitrary obstacles that are thrown into their paths.

The central role of the entrepreneur in driving the entrepreneurial process is illustrated in Figure 6.1. An individual is needed who can both dream and do. He/she must be able to fill multiple roles and demonstrate multiple characteristics. These include visionary, leader, promoter, risk-taker, leverager of resources, networker, and adapter. This individual is responsible for developing, adapting, or adopting a business concept. As discussed in Chapters 3 and 4, concepts can take any number of shapes or forms and will vary in terms of their innovativeness, riskiness, and level of proactiveness required. He/she implements the business concept within some type of organizational context. It might be a sole proprietorship run out of the person's garage at home, a franchise, or a venture team operating within a billion-dollar corporation. Finally, he/she must ensure that there is a fit between the business concept and the opportunity. The opportunity is defined by forces in the environment (e.g., the market, competi-

Figure 6.1
The Entrepreneur as Driving Force

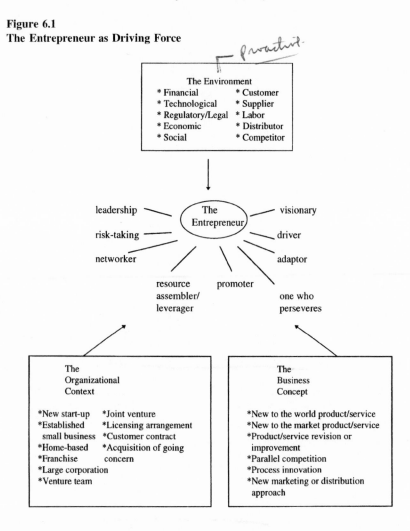

tion, technology). The environment is also a source of various threats and obstacles, which the entrepreneur must be prepared to address (see Chapter 5).

The characteristics and skills that determine the successfulness of the entrepreneurial venture will differ, depending upon the nature of the business concept, the organizational context, and the environment. Willingness and ability to assume and manage risks are more critical with truly new-to-the-world products. Political skills become crucial in large corporate settings. Adaptability and tenacity may be bigger factors in highly turbulent environments. At the same time, certain traits are fairly consistently associated with entrepreneurial personality. Let us further explore this controversial issue.

THE ENTREPRENEURIAL PERSONALITY

The single most researched question within the field of entrepreneurship is, "Who is the entrepreneur?" A variety of sometimes conflicting findings exist regarding the sociology and psychology of the entrepreneurial prototype. Many of these studies suffer from significant methodological problems. Samples are often small or unrepresentative. The validity and reliability of the measures employed are frequently not apparent, measures are applied long after the individual has done anything entrepreneurial, and it is often not clear if the researchers are focusing only on successful entrepreneurs, on people who have started small businesses, on people who identify themselves as entrepreneurs, or on some other delimiter.

Nonetheless, there do appear to be some characteristics around which a consensus has emerged. On the sociological side, immigrant populations appear to produce more entrepreneurship per capita than non-immigrant populations, perhaps because they face a greater struggle to fit into society. Of course, the very fact that they immigrated suggests an opportunistic mind-set. Another finding concerns birth order within families. While it is a controversial issue, some have argued that first-born children more frequently pursue an entrepreneurial path, than do second- or third-born children, possibly because they are given more responsibility, confront more discipline, and deal with more ambiguity than their siblings (Bird, 1989). Other research suggests age is a factor, with some people arguing that successful entrepreneurs tend to be younger (Sexton and Van Auken, 1982), and others indicating that milestone years (e.g., ages 20, 25, 30, 35) exist, when individuals are more likely to do something entrepreneurial (Ronstadt, 1984). Age is, of course, correlated with education and experience. The average education level of entrepreneurs has increased over the past two decades, although disagreement exists as to whether entrepreneurs differ significantly from managers in terms of their educational backgrounds. Nonetheless, successful entrepreneurs tend to have more education than their less successful counterparts (Sexton and Van Auken, 1982). Work experience, also, has more to do with predicting entrepreneurial success than with distinguishing entrepreneurs from non-entrepreneurs (Bird, 1989).

On the psychological side, there is some agreement on at least six characteristics (see Table 6.1 for a more comprehensive list of psychological traits associated with the entrepreneurial personality). Let us start with motivation. Entrepreneurs are driven by a variety of factors, ranging from necessity (I need to survive!) to dissatisfaction (I can't stand my present job) to curiosity (What if . . . ?) to material gain (We could make a killing!) to happenstance (Here's an opportunity if you want it). Yet, based on the classic studies of motivation done by McClelland, in which he assessed three fundamental types of motivators (power, affiliation, and achievement), the research evidence identifies entrepreneurs as being more achievement-motivated than anything else. They are driven

Table 6.1
Seventeen Common Traits and Characteristics Associated with the
Entrepreneurial Individual

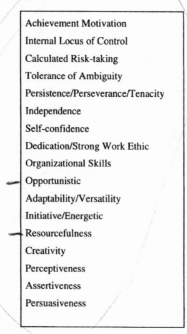

Achievement Motivation

Internal Locus of Control

Calculated Risk-taking

Tolerance of Ambiguity

Persistence/Perseverance/Tenacity

Independence

Self-confidence

Dedication/Strong Work Ethic

Organizational Skills

Opportunistic

Adaptability/Versatility

Initiative/Energetic

Resourcefulness

Creativity

Perceptiveness

Assertiveness

Persuasiveness

by the task, the challenge, the opportunity to accomplish what others said could not, would not, or should not be done. Money certainly counts, but it is a by-product. Money serves as a score card, telling the entrepreneur that he or she is making progress.

Second, entrepreneurial individuals demonstrate a strong internal locus of control. Unlike those who believe that external events control their lives and dictate what happens around them, entrepreneurs are change agents. They fundamentally believe that, with enough time and effort and their own involvement, they can change their workplace, their markets, their industries—in short, their environments.

Third, entrepreneurial individuals are calculated risk-takers. The entrepreneur tends to be about a 5.5 on a 10-point scale, where 1 = "risk avoidant" and 10 = "bold gambler." Calculated risk-taking can be defined as pursuit of a course of action that has a reasonable chance of costly failure, where failure is a significant negative difference between anticipated and actual results. It is calculated in the sense that (a) the individual has considered and attempted to estimate (at least conceptually) the likelihood and magnitude of the key risk factors; and

(b) he/she has attempted to manage or mitigate the key risk factors through good planning and managerial decision making.

Fourth, the very nature of the entrepreneurial process demands that the entrepreneur demonstrate a high "tolerance of ambiguity." Things do not have to be precise, fit a precast mold or follow an exact process. The process will inherently be loose, messy, and can abruptly move in new and unanticipated directions. Few entrepreneurs find that their successful business concept is an exact replica of their original idea. Few ventures unfold in the manner described in the original business plan. This is not because of poor conceptualizing or planning; it is the fundamental nature of the game. Even in the case of a franchise purchase, where there may be less risk-taking and innovativeness, ambiguities are likely in dealings with financiers, suppliers and service providers, and in the marketplace.

Fifth, entrepreneurs tend to prize their independence. They are self-motivated, self-reliant, and prefer a degree of autonomy when accomplishing a task. The perception that they have room to maneuver in affecting their own destiny is highly valued. Finally, it is generally agreed that entrepreneurs are tenacious and demonstrate significant perseverance.

Other common findings, about which there is less consensus, suggest that entrepreneurs are versatile, persuasive, creative, well-organized, extremely hard-working, and competitive (need to win).

According to some observers, there is also a "dark side" to entrepreneurs. Kets de Vries (1984) argues that many entrepreneurs have an excessive need for control, which may produce a tendency to micro-manage or do other people's jobs for them. They can also demonstrate a tendency toward suspicious thinking that goes beyond thinking someone will steal their concept. Other characteristics include impatience, a need for applause, seeing the world in terms of black and white, defensiveness, and the externalizing of internal problems.

As indicated earlier, our position is that entrepreneurs are not born, nor can someone simply be taught to be entrepreneurial. Although filled with controversy, the research on entrepreneurial characteristics makes one thing clear. The traits associated with entrepreneurial behavior are strongly influenced by the environment (see Chapter Five) and are developed over time. The list of traits and characteristics in Table 6.1 does not contain items that are clearly genetic, such as intelligence, physical prowess, or artistic talent. The tendencies to be self-confident, to have an internal locus of control, and to be achievement motivated, and similar attributes are the result of family, educational, social, and work experiences. Further, there is some entrepreneurial potential in each and every one of us.

Bird (1989) has provided an excellent illustration of the environmental perspective applied at the level of the individual. She synthesizes a wide array of findings from the literature to demonstrate how the prototypical entrepreneur is the product of specific developments in his/her social, economic, and family environments. This synthesis appears in Table 6.2. At the same time, Bird's perspective, and the perspective presented up to this point, implies the existence of a single prototype of the entrepreneur. As we shall see, there are, in fact, different types of entrepreneurs.

CATEGORIES OF ENTREPRENEURS

One of the earliest attempts to identify types or categories of entrepreneurs involved distinguishing "craftsmen" from "opportunists" (Smith, 1967). Craftsmen are characterized by narrowness in education and training, blue-collar origins, low social awareness and involvement, a feeling of inadequacy in dealing with the social environment, and a limited time orientation. They create businesses of a more rigid nature. Alternatively, opportunistic entrepreneurs exhibit breadth in education and training, middle-class origins, a variety of work experiences, high social awareness and involvement, confidence in their ability to deal with the social environment, and an awareness of, and orientation towards, the future. They are more likely to create organizations that are adaptable to change and growth-oriented.

Kets de Vries (1977) adds a third category of entrepreneur, the Research and Development (R + D) or technical entrepreneur. These individuals often, but not always, come up with their own inventions or product modifications. They typically have work experience in a high technology environment, have a more formal technical education, and make greater use of teams.

A distinction somewhat similar to the one above is made by Kao (1991), who discusses "creative or charismatic" and "conventional" entrepreneurs. The former tend to do something that is more innovative and has a higher risk profile, while the latter build a venture around existing (or slightly improved) products or services. As well, the former are often more growth-oriented than the latter.

In examining why some entrepreneurs succeed in one type of venture and fail in another, and why some succeed initially but fail once a venture reaches a certain size, Miner (1996) concludes that four different types of entrepreneurs exist, each of which achieves success by approaching entrepreneurship from a different route. These include:

The Personal Achiever (the classic entrepreneur):

• high need for achievement

• need for performance feedback

• desire to plan and set goals

• strong individual initiative

• strong personal commitment and identification with their organization

• internal locus of control

• belief that work should be guided by personal goals, not those of others

Table 6.2
A Psychoanalytic Model of Entrepreneurship

Social, cultural, historic, economic context

Society that supports the development of authoritarian personality Family poverty

AND

Childhood family dynamics

Father's: Absence   Mother's: Dominance
        Remoteness   Nurturance
        Villainy
        Role-model

RESULT IN

Disrupted, deprived childhood Conflicts in identification (love-hate) Splitting the good and bad (either-or thinking, closed-mindedness) Persistent feelings of dissatisfaction, rejection, powerlessness, low self-esteem, distrust

THAT DEVELOP INTO

Young adulthood characterized by

Disorientation, goal-lessness, testing Non-conformity, rebelliousness Enjoying setbacks (martyrdom, masochism) High need for control Suspicious thinking Fear of being victimized Scanning the environment

THROUGH A SERIES OF CONSCIOUS CHOICES A PERSON ENDS UP AS AN ENTREPRENEUR

Adulthood creation of an organization that is

Authoritarian Centralized Lacking trust and delegation Lacking planning, impulsive A work environment of high dependency and power that is a function of centrality or closeness to the entrepreneur Unresolved regarding succession: Rivalry with sons   Coping with loss or losing control

Source: Bird (1989).

The Super-Salesperson (follows the selling route to success, caters to the needs of customers)
- capacity to understand and feel with another, to empathize
- desire to help others
- belief that social processes are important; social interaction and relationships are important
- need to have strong positive relationships with others
- belief that the salesforce is crucial to carrying out company strategy
- background of fewer years of education and more years of business experience, and especially selling experience, than other entrepreneurs

The Real Manager (unless he/she overmanages the early stage venture, is able to grow the venture significantly)
- desire to be a corporate leader
- desire to compete
- decisiveness
- desire for power
- positive attitudes to authority
- desire to stand out from the crowd

The Expert Idea Generator (expertise plus creativity = innovator)
- desire to innovate
- love of ideas, curious, open-minded
- belief that new product development is crucial component of company strategy
- good intelligence; thinking is at center of their entrepreneurial approach; intelligence as a source of competitive advantage
- desire to avoid taking risks

Some people are likely to demonstrate patterns that fit into more than one of these categories. Miner (1996) argues that these individuals can succeed by pursuing more than one route. For others, however, their success is dependent on pursuing an approach to entrepreneurship consistent with the dominant pattern into which they fall.

An alternative typology, proposed by Vesper (1980), looks not at the characteristics of the person, but instead, at the method they rely upon to build their venture. He identifies ten types of entrepreneurs:

1. *Solo self-employed*: Includes Mom and Pop stores, professionals, and trades people who work alone or with very few people, and who do most of the work themselves.

2. *Team builders*: People who build an organization through incremental hiring.

3. *Independent innovators*: Inventors who build an organization to produce and sell an invention; they may build a high-technology organization.

4. *Pattern multipliers*: People who expand a business concept through franchises or chains of similar stores.

5. *Economy of scale exploiters*: People who increase volume and lower price by large-scale production or sales.

6. *Acquirers*: People who purchase or inherit a going concern.

7. *Buy-sell artists*: Those who buy companies to later resell them at a profit: turnaround artists, corporate raiders, and take-over experts.

8. *Conglomerators*: Variation of acquirers: those who use the assets of one company to buy control of others not necessarily related to the first business.

9. *Speculators*: People who purchase an asset such as land to leverage the purchase of other assets (more land, construction); resell later at a profit.

10. *Apparent value manipulators*: The "buy low, sell high entrepreneur," the classic "arbitrageur": those who repackage, redefine, or restructure to add apparent value.

In conclusion, there has been little research on the identification of categories of entrepreneurs, and the research that has been done suffers from methodological limitations. Even so, there is strong reason to believe that multiple types exist, and that entrepreneurs can differ in terms of their relative risk profiles, sources of motivation, managerial capabilities, and other characteristics.

THE PATHS TO ENTREPRENEURSHIP: TRIGGERING EVENTS

The term "entrepreneur" is a label. It has been applied fairly indiscriminately to describe small business owners, industry pioneers, inventors, corporate turn-around artists, dynamic leaders, those who creatively engineer take-overs or buyouts, and builders of large conglomerates. These days, it is applied to people who start political and religious movements, instigate major social changes, or remake nations. To be designated an entrepreneur is usually considered a positive attribution, suggesting one has successfully built something more from something less. However, success is not a necessary ingredient, for many entrepreneurs fail.

Yet most of those individuals that we think of as entrepreneurs did not wake up one morning and say to themselves, "I think I'll be an entrepreneur." (Ironically, many of them do not consider themselves entrepreneurs even after they have achieved great success.) The paths that they take are as different as the stars in the sky. They may start early or late in life or do entrepreneurial things throughout their lives. Some pursue the path deliberately; others find themselves there due to circumstances. Some begin with a vision; others develop one along the way. One may start with a single goal and, once it is accomplished, aim for a bigger goal. Another begins with a grand objective and will settle for nothing less. Some are luckier than others, and some work much harder than others.

While there is no formula or recipe that entrepreneurs follow, many start down the path because of some "triggering event." Table 6.3 provides thirteen examples of entrepreneurial triggers. This is not an exhaustive list but does highlight most of the major factors that ultimately cause the individual to "go for it" at a particular point in time. It is interesting to note that all of the triggers in Table 6.3 except "deliberate search" are the result of circumstances or developments in the environment.

Table 6.3
Thirteen Entrepreneurial Triggers

Negative Triggers	Illustration
Survival	"My current situation does not pay the rent"
Job dissatisfaction	"I hate my boss, my work, my environment"
Lay-off or retrenchment	"My employer no longer needs me"
Business in trouble	"We lost a key account, technology has made us obsolete, costs are through the roof, our major supplier dropped us . . . we've got to do something"
Divorce	"I'm suddenly on my own with no source of support"
Death	"Dad died unexpectedly and left me with a troubled business that I had to turn around"
Positive Triggers	
Fresh start	"I just graduated from school, or just moved to a new place, and am ready to do something different
Opportunity knocks	"My employer offered to finance me if I would become his outsourced supplier" (or) "A customer promised me a huge order if I could develop a widget for him"
Curiosity	"What if . . . I saw something that intrigued me and just decided to give it a go"
Desire to improve one's lot	"I wanted to take control of my life and put myself in a situation where my own efforts determined my returns"
Now or never	"I turned forty, realized I'm not getting any younger and decided to go for it"
Windfall	"I won the lottery or inherited a bundle from Aunt Betty, and decided to do something positive with it"
Deliberate Search	"I've always known I would do something entrepreneurial, I just needed to find the right opportunity"

Consider Dino Cortopassi, a farmer in Northern California. Dino, whose father was also a farmer, found that he had no strategic leverage when it came to marketing his cherries, tomatoes, and other farm products. He was a price taker, and could basically sell whatever he produced at going market rates, which fluctuated considerably based on aggregate supply and demand conditions. No matter how large or efficient he got, margins were uncontrollable, and returns on a sizable fixed investment were often dismal. Faced with these circumstances, he decided to move downstream and get into food processing. Dino pioneered the branding of what many considered to be a commodity—the tomato. Today, his San Tomo Group is a leading marketer of high quality, branded tomato by-products, such as tomato paste and tomato sauces. San Tomo products are used in many of the best restaurants in North America.

Consider the list of triggers in Table 6.3. Dino wanted room to maneuver in determining his own destiny. He would therefore be an example of "desire to improve one's lot," although some of the other triggers may also have been operating.

While we have grouped the triggering factors in Table 6.3 into positive and negative, another perspective is to distinguish between "push" and "pull" factors (Phillips and Brice, 1988). One is pushed into entrepreneurship by unemployment or job dissatisfaction. One is pulled by the perception of market opportunities, the receipt of an economic windfall, or the desire to mimic some role model. Unfortunately, the available research findings regarding whether success rates differ based on whether one is pushed or pulled are mixed.

THE ROLE OF TEAMS

Up to this point, we have argued that entrepreneurship does not happen without entrepreneurs. Just as important is the need to recognize that successful entrepreneurship does not happen without teams.

In the contemporary environment, new ventures are frequently built around a mix of technologies; interdependent methods of production, inventory management, supplier relationships, and logistics; relatively complicated financing schemes; leveraged assets that are not easy to control; customization of products and communications to different market segments or individual clients; and a mix of regular and contract employees as well as full- and part-time employees. Getting things done properly and on a timely basis is dependent on a skilled and well-integrated team. Further, the entrepreneurial process is lengthy and filled with obstacles, suggesting the need for a motivated, coordinated group of individuals, each having his/her own contributions to make.

It becomes necessary to reconcile the concept of individualism, which we intimately associate with entrepreneurial behavior, with the concept of the team, group, or collective, which is also a necessity. Individualism refers to a self-orientation, an emphasis on self-sufficiency and control, the pursuit of individual goals that may or may not be consistent with those of one's colleagues or associates, and a value system where people derive pride from their own accomplishments. A group or collective orientation involves the subordination of personal interests to the goals of the larger work group, an emphasis on sharing, cooperation, and group harmony, a concern with group welfare, and antipathy towards those outside the group.

In a work context, there are positive and negative aspects to both individualism and a group or collective orientation. Table 6.4 provides a summary of these pros and cons. In essence, an individualistic ethic may foster development of an individual's self-confidence, lead to a greater sense of personal responsibility, create more of a competitive spirit, and produce higher-risk, breakthrough innovations. It can also produce selfishness, high levels of stress, and interper-

Table 6.4
Individualism versus a Group or Collective Orientation

Individualism	Group or Collective Orientation
Pros: • Employee develops stronger self-concept, more self-confidence • Consistent with achievement motivation • Competition among individuals encourages greater numbers of novel concepts and ideas; breakthrough innovations • Stronger sense of personal responsibility for performance outcomes • Linkage between personal effort and rewards creates greater sense of equity Cons: • Emphasis on personal gain at expense of others, selfishness, materialism • Individuals have less commitment/loyalty, are more "up for sale" • Differences among individuals are emphasized • Interpersonal conflicts are encouraged • Greater levels of personal stress, pressure for individual performance • Insecurity can result from overdependence on oneself • Greater feelings of loneliness, alienation, and anomie • Stronger incentive for unethical behaviour, expediency • Onus of failure falls on the individual	Pros: • Greater synergies from combined efforts of people with differing skills • Ability to incorporate diverse perspectives and achieve comprehensive view • Individuals treated as equals • Relationships more personalized, synchronized, harmonious, while interpersonal conflicts are discouraged • Greater concern for welfare of others, network of social support available • More consensus regarding direction and priorities • Credit for failures and successes equally shared • Teamwork produces steady, incremental progress on projects Cons: • Loss of personal and professional self to group/collective • Greater emotional dependence on individuals in the group or organization • Less personal responsibility for outcomes • Individuals "free ride" on efforts of others, rewards not commensurate with effort • Tendency toward "group think" • Outcomes can represent compromises among diverse interests, reflecting need to get along more than need for performance • Collectives can take more time to reach consensus, may miss opportunities

sonal conflict. A group orientation offers the advantages of more harmonious relationships between individuals, greater synergies, more social support, and can result in a steady stream of incremental improvements and innovations. On the downside, the team or group focus can entail the loss of individual identity, greater emotional dependency, a tendency to "free ride" on the efforts of others, compromises rather than optimizing behavior, and "group think," in which individuals get locked into a singular shared way of viewing or approaching a problem.

The ability to start, grow, and sustain any entrepreneurial venture requires a balance between the need for individual initiative and the spirit of cooperation and group ownership of innovation. This balance is pictured in Figure 6.2. As the entrepreneurial process unfolds, the individual champion requires not just specialist expertise, but teams of people, some of whom can fill multiple roles. Members of these teams are able to collaborate in meeting tight timelines, identifying and overcoming unanticipated obstacles, and finding angles and opportunities that often redefine the entrepreneur's concept, putting it on a more successful path. Sometimes it is the entrepreneur who keeps the team on track, and other times it is the team that is the voice of reason and consistency.

NETWORKS AND THE ENTREPRENEUR

In addition to internal teams, every entrepreneur is dependent on external networks (corporate entrepreneurs actually have a network that consists of both

Figure 6.2
The Relationship between Entrepreneurship and an Emphasis on the Individual versus the Group or Collective

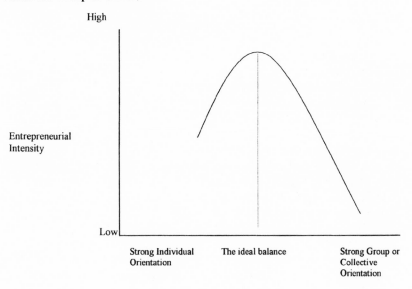

internal and external elements). The entrepreneur's networking abilities and the quality of the network he/she builds often define the ultimate level of success achieved by the venture.

The term "network" is used to describe a number of people and organizations that are connected. They are formed for a variety of purposes but, in this case, to facilitate some form of economic exchange. The network approach emphasizes the dynamic ability of the entrepreneur to shift and switch among the resources used in the venture. Three major benefits result from a good network:

- Empowerment—through the network, the entrepreneur is able to gain access to resources that he/she would not otherwise have; the entrepreneur can achieve reach, power, and economies of scale.

- Predictability—networks result in long-term relationships that reduce the uncertainty surrounding whether and when the entrepreneur can obtain assistance and where to go for that assistance.

- Expanded scope and focus—in addition to providing resources for current operations, the network is a vehicle for recognizing and capitalizing on opportunities the entrepreneur would otherwise have missed.

Networks can be characterized in terms of their diversity, density, reachability, and the value of each member (Dubini and Aldrich, 1991). *Diversity* is a reflection of the variety of those who make up the network. A non-diverse network might consist only of one's close acquaintances. A diverse network might include casual and close acquaintances, strangers, company representatives, government officials, an interactive Internet site, and much more. *Density* refers to the extensiveness of ties between the various network members. These ties can be absent or present, weak or strong. In dense networks, individuals are all aware of one another, and information and resources are rapidly and efficiently transferred within the network. *Reachability* is concerned with the path between two persons or organizations. Can a given member of the network be reached directly, only through an intermediary or perhaps two intermediaries, or is the person fairly isolated? *Value* is a reflection of a member's contribution to the entrepreneur's network. It attempts to capture how useful or critical a role the member plays. A member generates value through the information he/she provides, through non-informational resources (e.g., money, office space, advice), or through the linkages he/she provides to other members of the network.

A valuable component of any network is the presence of brokers. These are people that enable the entrepreneur to leverage his/her effectiveness by using available knowledge to access more effective resource providers. Thus, brokers do not provide resources directly, they provide access. Brokers essentially facilitate the interests of entrepreneurs who are not directly connected to the best resource providers.

To see a network in action, let's consider an example of an entrepreneur and the start-up process she went through (Figure 6.3). Her firm operates tours for

Figure 6.3
An Illustration of an Entrepreneur's Network: The Case of a Tour Operator

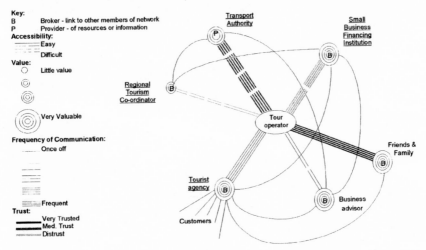

international and local visitors into black townships in South Africa. She has a technical diploma and previous work experience related to the venture she was starting up. At the start-up of her venture, she had only her house and a small personal savings account at the bank. So at face value, her resources appear extremely limited.

Our entrepreneur's original job was with a tourist agency, and through her strong relationship with them, and their knowledge of the industry, she was able to establish her company with very few resources of her own. She even got the telephone company to install her telephone without any down payment required. The links in the network she developed represent sets of relationships. These relationships can be characterized not only by their of accessibility, value, and the frequency of communication, but also by the level of trust that develops between her and the other party. Trust is the key underlying variable that determines how solid and permanent a given link in the network is. In effect, a network allows our entrepreneur to expand her circle of trust.

Her network formation efforts are graphically represented in the diagram above. Her previous employer acted as a broker in her network formation efforts, by connecting her with a sophisticated business advisor, as well as referring her services to potential customers. This advisor, with whom she had a short, extremely valuable, one time, but trusting connection, put her in contact with a small business financing institution as well as a transport authority. From the finance institution she received funds, and from the transport authority she managed to negotiate to use the local public transport vehicles and their drivers during off-peak hours. This relationship with the transport authority enabled her to provide a service to her customers in authentic local transport without having to make any long-term commitment.

The density of her network implies that a high level of trust runs throughout her entire set of relationships and indicates how she was able to quickly arrive at effective sources of resources to capitalize on her opportunity. The network also facilitated rapid information and resource transfer. The presence of valuable members indicates that each was used to his/her fullest potential with the highest level of cooperation and the greatest possible economic benefit derived. A possible limitation to her network is its reachability; her network has essentially not extended beyond that which she had developed at start-up. This should be the focus of future development efforts.

Entrepreneurs should keep in mind that the ultimate goal of all the members of a network is to achieve common goals. Emphasizing mutually beneficial relationships can lead the entrepreneur to recognize new opportunities as well as improve the quality of day-to-day business decisions. Entrepreneurs can better conceptualize their positions within a network and seek ways to harness potential benefits and opportunities that arise out of network cooperation. Individuals with limited resources can use their networks to significantly leverage their positions by tapping into the resources of others.

In the final analysis, by forming strategic alliances and broadening the reach of their network during the start-up phase of a new venture, entrepreneurs significantly increase the likelihood of survival and growth. In fact, advice on creating and managing external networks may actually prove more valuable in the long run than advice on how to run the business itself.

CONCLUSIONS

Entrepreneurship is a bottom-up process. It does not start with government policy or corporate strategy. It begins with people. The modern history of the entrepreneur has focused on special people who stand out from the crowd. Our argument is that the focus should actually be on ordinary people who do special things. Stated differently, everybody has some level of entrepreneurial potential.

A related conclusion is that there is no single prototype of the entrepreneur. There may be some general traits that entrepreneurs tend to have more in common than do corporate managers, government administrators, blue-collar workers, or other groups. Yet, entrepreneurs vary in terms of these traits, and some are strong on other traits that are not generally associated with the "classic" entrepreneur. As a result, four or five general categories of entrepreneurs emerge.

Finally, the culture of entrepreneurship is assumed to be rooted in a tradition of individualism. We believe individualism is vital and question those who would abandon the individual in favor of the group or collective. Even so, rarely does the entrepreneurial concept succeed without a devoted team and a supportive network. Teams will vary in their nature and scope, but they are indispensable. Some play more of a strategic role, and others are more operational. In some organizations, the entrepreneur is a co-equal team participant, while in others he/she is dictatorial and the team follows and implements. Similarly, networks provide a vehicle for entrepreneurs to do more, do it faster, and achieve higher quality levels. There is a need in most entrepreneurial ventures for an explicit "networking strategy," which should cover such issues as the size and membership of one's network, the roles to be played, the frequency and types of communication with members, the types of mutual benefits to be created, and the methods of building trust.

In deciding what is an appropriate level of entrepreneurial intensity in one's life, individuals must balance frequency of entrepreneurial activity against degree. Further, they must balance their own risk-taking profile and innovativeness against their personal responsibilities and lifestyle choices, as well as against their personal abilities to build, motivate, and work with teams and networks.

REFERENCES

Bird, B.J. 1989. *Entrepreneurial Behavior*. London: Scott, Foresman.

Dubini, P., and Aldrich, H. 1991. "Personal and Extended Networks are Central to the Entrepreneurial Process." *Journal of Business Venturing*, 6, 305–313.

Kao, J.J. 1991. *The Entrepreneur*. Englewood Cliffs, NJ: Prentice-Hall.

Kets de Vries, M.F.R. 1977. "The Entrepreneurial Personality: A Person at the Crossroads." *Journal of Management Studies*, 14, 34–57.

Kets de Vries, M.F.R. 1984. *Can You Survive an Entrepreneur?* Boston: HBS Case Services.

McClelland, D. 1987. "Characteristics of Successful Entrepreneurs." *Journal of Creative Behavior*, 21, 219–233.

Miner, J.B. 1996. *The 4 Routes to Entrepreneurial Success*. San Francisco: Berrett-Koehler Publishers.

Phillips, B., and Brice, H. 1988. "Black Business in South Africa: A Challenge to Enterprise." *International Journal of Small Business*, 6 (3), 42–58.

Ronstadt, R.C. 1984. *Entrepreneurship: Text, Cases and Notes*. Dover, MA: Lord Publishing.

Sexton, D.L., and Van Auken, P.M. 1982. *Successful vs. Unsuccessful Entrepreneurs: A Comparative Study*. Paper presented at the Babson College Entrepreneurship Research Conference.

Smith, N.R. 1967. *The Entrepreneur and His Firm: The Relationship between Type of Man and Type of Company*. Lansing, MI: Bureau of Business and Economic Research, Graduate School of Business Administration, Michigan State University.

Vesper, K. 1980. *New Venture Strategies*. Englewood Cliffs, NJ: Prentice-Hall.

7

The Entrepreneurial Organization

INTRODUCTION

Organizations can be characterized in terms of their overall strategic orientation. A key aspect of this orientation concerns entrepreneurship. As we saw in Chapter 4, organizations differ significantly in terms of the level of entrepreneurial intensity (EI) that they demonstrate. The entrepreneurial organization is one in which managers are more inclined to take business-related risks, to favor innovation and change in advancing the organization's interests, and to anticipate and preemptorily respond to the actions of suppliers, competitors, customers, and other publics.

Achieving an entrepreneurial orientation is not something that management can simply decide to do. It requires considerable time and investment, and there must be continual reinforcement. As we shall see, the typical organization imposes significant constraints on entrepreneurial behavior. To be sustainable, the entrepreneurial spirit must be integrated into the mission, goals, strategies, structure, processes, and values of the organization.

The importance of entrepreneurship in a corporate context is primarily environmentally determined. Where the external environments of corporations are characterized as increasingly dynamic, threatening, or complex, managers find themselves losing control over these environments. The appropriate strategies for addressing such environmental turbulence can be generally grouped into two categories: adaptive and entrepreneurial.

The adaptive approach is to anticipate environmental change, and then quickly adjust to the changing conditions, or buffer the firm to limit its vulnerability. Organizational survival is a function both of a firm's speed in responding to change and of its ability to establish defensive barriers to moderate the impact of significant environmental developments.

Although widely accepted, this is an overly passive and reactive point of view. The survival of firms as we move into the twenty-first century may well depend on their ability to manage the environment and to serve as agents of change. Such firms will seek to continually rewrite the rules of the competitive game. This is the entrepreneurial approach.

MANAGERS AS PROMOTERS VERSUS TRUSTEES

An extremely useful perspective that can be applied to organizational entrepreneurship is provided by Stevenson and colleagues (1994). As summarized in Figure 7.1, they suggest that a business can be characterized in terms of six key dimensions: the company's strategic orientation, commitment to opportunity, methods for making resource commitments, strategies for controlling resources, organizational structure, and approach to rewards. A further distinction can be drawn between the manager as "promoter" and the manager as "trustee." A promoter adopts an entrepreneurial approach to management, focuses on the pursuit of opportunity, and promotes change. A trustee is at the other end of the continuum, and is someone primarily concerned with efficient utilization of the resources under his/her control. A more complete comparison of promoters and trustees can be found in Table 7.1.

In essence, the entrepreneurial organization has managers who wear the "promoter" hat far more often than the "trustee" hat. These organizations design strategies that are opportunity-driven rather than resource-driven; they make revolutionary commitments to new opportunities, capitalize on a given opportunity, and then move on to the next one. Their resource commitments are multi-staged, with minimal exposure at each stage; these resources are leveraged, leased, rented, or contracted; the organizational structure is flat with informal networks; and the reward system is based on value created with no limits on what a person or team can potentially earn.

The other significant contribution of the Stevenson framework concerns the identification of factors creating a need for more entrepreneurial (promoter) versus administrative (trustee) approaches to managing the organization. The authors imply that EI becomes more critical as organizations find their opportunity streams diminishing and external environments changing faster. Further, short decision windows, limited decision constituencies, lack of predictable resource needs, an inability to control internal and external developments, pressures for more opportunity per resource unit, and employee demands for more independence are all factors that force organizations to become more entrepreneurial.

For many large, established firms, the pressures from each of these can be expected to magnify in the foreseeable future. In fact, much of the current interest in facilitating corporate entrepreneurship originates from companies facing these very pressures. Furthermore, there is a small but growing volume of

Figure 7.1
Key Business Dimensions and Entrepreneurship

Pressures toward this side	Promoter	Key Business Dimension	Trustee	Pressures toward this side
Diminished opportunity streams Rapidly changing: technology, consumer economics, social values	Driven by perception of opportunity	**Strategic orientation** ← Entrepreneurial domain → Administrative domain	Driven by resources currently controlled	Social contracts Performance-measurement criteria Planning systems and cycle
Action orientation Short decision windows Risk management Limited decision constituencies	Revolutionary with short duration	**Commitment to opportunity** ← Entrepreneurial domain → Administrative domain	Evolutionary of long duration	Acknowledgement of multiple constituencies Negotiation of strategy Risk reduction Management of fit
Lack of predictable resource needs Lack of long-term control Social need for more opportunity per resource unit Interpersonal pressure for more efficient resource use	Multi-staged with minimal exposure at each stage	**Commitment of Resources** ← Entrepreneurial domain → Administrative domain	Single-staged with complete commitment upon decision	Personal risk reduction Incentive compensation Managerial turnover Capital allocation systems Formal planning systems
Increased resource specialization Long resource life compared to need Risk obsolescence Risk inherent in any new venture Inflexibility of permanent commitment to resources	Episodic use or rent of required resources	**Control of Resources** ← Entrepreneurial domain → Administrative domain	Ownership or employment of required resources	Power, status and financial rewards Coordination Efficiency measures Inertia and cost of change Industry structures
Coordination of key non-controlled resources Challenge to legitimacy of owner's control Employees' desire for independence	Flat with multiple informal networks	**Management Structure** ← Entrepreneurial domain → Administrative domain	Formalized hierarchy	Need for clearly defined authority and responsibility Organizational culture Reward systems Management theory
Individual expectations Competition Increased perception of personal wealth-creation possibilities	Value-based Team-based Unlimited	**Compensation/ Reward Policy** ← Entrepreneurial domain → Administrative domain	Resource-based Driven by short-term data Promotion Limited amount	Societal norms Tax regulations Impacted information Search for simple solutions for complex problems Demands on public shareholders

Source: Stevenson et al. (1994). Reprinted with permission.

Table 7.1
Promoters and Trustees

The Manager as **PROMOTER** (entrepreneur)
• Confident of his/her ability to seize opportunity
• Expects surprises
• Adjusts to and capitalizes on change
• Flexible -- can move from project to project, team to team, division to division
• Proactive, makes things happen; believes in own ability to effect change
• Opportunity-driven rather than resource-driven; pursues opportunity regardless of resources currently controlled
• Calculated risk-taker
• Externally-focused
• Views failure as valuable learning experience
• Less concerned with long-term job security -- more concerned with autonomy and freedom
The Manager as **TRUSTEE** (administrator)
• Threatened by change
• Cautious, emphasizes maintenance of status quo
• Stresses predictability, relies on conventional wisdom and rules of thumb
• Concentrates on efficiency in utilizing resources
• Resource-driven, not opportunity-driven
• Risk-aversive
• Reactive
• Internally-focused
• Concerned with job security, power, position

empirical research supporting the need for more entrepreneurial management. Miller and Friesen (1983), for instance, have found a significant positive relationship between the degree of environmental dynamism, hostility, and heterogeneity present and the amount of proactive, risk-taking, and innovative behavior in successful firms. They found no such relationship, however, in unsuccessful firms (see also Morris and Sexton, 1996).

EFFECTING CHANGE: WHERE TO FOCUS ATTENTION

Organizations tend to evolve through different stages as they grow and mature (Adizes, 1978; Griener, 1972). The requirements of size are such that developing firms go through a metamorphosis in moving from start-up venture to large diversified corporation. Stated differently, large companies are not simply scaled-up versions of small companies. While many small enterprises fail to demonstrate significant entrepreneurship, the constraints on entrepreneurship in such firms are comparatively limited. However, the changes instituted or experienced by larger companies to accommodate growth also tend to undermine the potential for ongoing entrepreneurship in these firms (Knight, 1987; Stefflre, 1985).

While the actual constraints on corporate entrepreneurship derive from many sources, they can be generally classified into six groups: systems, structure, strategic direction, policies, people, and culture. This framework is proposed based on an extensive review of the limited literature on corporate entrepreneurship, surveys of a number of medium-size and large industrial organizations, and in-depth assessments of three Fortune 500 companies.

Examples of the specific constraints found within each group are provided in Table 7.2. This set of items is not an exhaustive list but instead includes some of the more pervasive problem areas. Also, the groups are not mutually exclusive or independent. For instance, systems overlap with policies, while people problems may be highly correlated with cultural problems. Keeping this interdependence in mind, let us examine each of the categories.

Systems

Maturing organizations are typically dependent upon a number of formal managerial systems that have evolved over the years. These systems seek to provide stability, order, and coordination to an increasingly complex internal corporate environment. The trade-off, however, is a strong disincentive for entrepreneurship.

For example, employee reward and measurement systems often encourage safe, conservative behavior and actions that produce short-term payoffs. Other

Table 7.2
Six Categories of Organizational Constraints on Entrepreneurship

Systems	Structures	Strategic Direction	Policies and Procedures	People	Culture
• Misdirected reward and evaluation systems • Oppressive control systems • Inflexible budgeting systems • Arbitrary cost allocation systems • Overly rigid, formal planning systems	• Too many hierarchical levels • Overly narrow span of control • Responsibility without authority • Top-down management • Restricted communication channels • Lack of accountability • Bloated staff functions	• Absence of innovation goals • No formal strategy for entrepreneurship • No vision from the top • Lack of commitment from senior executives • No entrepreneurial role models at the top	• Long, complex approval cycles • Extensive documentation requirements • Overreliance on established rules of thumb • Unrealistic performance criteria	• Fear of failure • Resistance to change • Parochial bias • "Turf" protection • Complacency • Short-term orientation • Inappropriate skills/talents	• Ill-defined values • Lack of consensus over priorities • Lack of fit • Values that conflict with entrepreneurial requirements

times, they are vague, inconsistent, or perceived as inequitable. Steven Kerr (1975) explains that many managers are guilty of the "folly of rewarding A, while hoping for B." They tend to ask for or expect innovative behavior, but actually measure and reward non-innovative behaviors. Control systems encourage managers to micro-manage the expenditure of every dollar and to establish quantifiable performance benchmarks in as many activity areas as possible. These benchmarks become ends in themselves. They also convey a lack of trust in employee discretion. Budgeting systems provide no flexibility for the funding of bootleg projects or experimentation and tend to reward the politically powerful. Costing systems are frequently based on arbitrary allocation schemes, where any product or project can be made to look untenable simply as a function of the indirect fixed costs that must be recovered.

Planning, although critical for successful entrepreneurship, often serves as an obstacle. This occurs because of an overemphasis on superfluous analysis, on form instead of content, on the document instead of the process, and on professional planners instead of having those charged with implementing the plan actually prepare the plan. The result is an overly rigid process that is incapable of quickly responding to new opportunities with short decision windows.

Structure

As a firm designs more hierarchical levels into the organizational structure, the ability to identify market opportunities, achieve management commitment, reallocate resources, take risks, or implement effective marketplace moves becomes problematic. Moreover, hierarchies tend to be accompanied by two other entrepreneurial barriers, top-down management and restrictive channels of communication. The result is frequently intransigence and a lack of commitment to innovation and change at all levels of the organization.

There is also a tendency to narrow the span of control of managers and to overdepartmentalize as firms mature. The result is oversupervised employees with little room to be creative or improvise. Furthermore, as employees become more segmented and compartmentalized, frames of reference become quite narrow. The ability to integrate perspectives and methods across boundaries is stifled. Meanwhile, accountability for effective change efforts is sufficiently diffused such that no one has a positive stake in ensuring that change occurs.

Structures that assign responsibility for entrepreneurial activities to managers, without commensurate authority, represent an additional constraint. Lacking the authority to try new methods or approaches to addressing obstacles, or to expend required resources, the manager is likely to become frustrated and perhaps cynical.

Strategic Direction

While the desire may be to achieve entrepreneurship throughout the firm, little can be accomplished without meaningful direction from the top. Established firms frequently have sophisticated planning systems that produce comprehensive strategies for marketing, production, and corporate finance but ignore the subject of innovation altogether. In the absence of specific goals for product and process innovation, and a strategy for accomplishing such goals, entrepreneurship will only result from happenstance.

More fundamental, however, is the lack of commitment from senior executives to the principle of institutionalized entrepreneurship. This requires leaders who are visionaries, seeing the firm and its people for what they can be, not what they have been. Instead, senior management is more typically cautious, suspicious, or completely unaware of efforts to break with tradition and capitalize on opportunity. Middle- and lower-level employees are strongly influenced by the role models found at the top of the organization. What they often find are politicians and technocrats, well-versed in the art of corporate survival.

Policies and Procedures

Those involved in entrepreneurial endeavours are, by definition, addressing the unknown. Their efforts are often undermined by organizational policies and procedures that were established to bring order and consistency to the everyday operational requirements of the firm. These requirements tend to be relatively well-known. Operating guidelines are established based on the rules of experience, with a premium placed on conservatism. The corporate entrepreneur comes to view these policies and procedures as burdensome red tape, and many find success to be unattainable unless rules are bent or broken.

Two of the most costly side-effects of detailed operating policies and procedures are complex approval cycles for new ventures and elaborate documentation requirements. These obstacles not only consume an inordinate amount of the entrepreneur's time and energy but frequently serve as well-designed mechanisms for incrementally dismantling an innovative concept.

A related problem is the tendency for existing policies and procedures to impose unrealistic timetables and performance benchmarks on entrepreneurial programs. This creates an incentive to compromise on truly novel ideas. The entrepreneur finds it necessary to tailor innovations to performance criteria that do not reflect changing competitive conditions.

People

Our research suggests that people are the greatest obstacle of all. The number-one priority in any attempt to increase the entrepreneurial intensity of an organization must be to change people, and specifically, to get them to be accepting of change and tolerant of failure in their own work. Entrepreneurship is concerned with change and the management of change efforts. There is, however, a natural tendency for people to resist change. Given the opportunity, employees become comfortable with established ways of doing things. They value predictability and stability and are frequently skeptical of the need for change.

Change is viewed as threatening and is met with a defensive, parochial attitude. This is especially the case where employees have no role in the change program.

There is, furthermore, a preoccupation among workers with the demands of the present, not the future. Correspondingly, it is unrealistic to expect them to adopt a long-term perspective or to recognize the need for continual adaptation.

The entrepreneurial spirit is additionally stifled by a pervading fear of failure that is prevalent in most companies. People come to believe it is better to avoid failure than to risk success. They apparently perceive there is more to lose than to gain. Not that failure must be congratulated; rather, it should be personally detested. But failure is an important medium for learning; it should be embraced as such. The reality is that a majority of new ventures (companies, products, services, processes) fail, suggesting the need for a realistic appraisal of the outcome of any entrepreneurial effort.

People motivation is also a problem, especially for those driven by a need for power and status. Such individuals approach questions of innovation from the standpoint of "turf protection." They hoard resources, especially information. They resist open communication and are suspicious of collaborative efforts.

One additional people-related issue concerns a general lack of skills and talents in the entrepreneurial area. While there is ample creative potential in every employee of the firm, many have never learned to develop or channel their creative energies. Some convince themselves that they are incapable of creative thinking. Others refuse to look beyond their current field of reference for ideas and solutions. Still others, on finding a creative solution, lack the skills necessary to bend the rules, build the coalitions, and work through or around the system to achieve successful implementation. Such problems are compounded by the apparent inability of many of those in supervisory positions to motivate and manage creative individuals.

Culture

Companies noted as successful innovators tend to foster a strong organizational culture. This culture is built around a central set of values that pervades every aspect of company operations. Employees are indoctrinated to internalize these values, and those who do not rarely last. These values are the lifeblood of the firm, creating the standards and providing the direction for growth and development.

Where companies fail to clearly define what they stand for, or do not achieve a consensus over value priorities (e.g., customer needs, quality, efficiency, service, reliability), entrepreneurship will have no focus. Even when priorities exist, values can be inconsistent with current competitive requirements. For instance, the company that stresses reliability or efficiency may find the marketplace puts a much higher premium on flexibility and value for the dollar.

Furthermore, entrepreneurship must itself become part of the organizational value system. This means company-wide commitment to innovation, calculated risk-taking, and proactiveness. Such a commitment becomes impossible when the pervading emphasis is on imitation of competitors, conservation, and self-aggrandizement.

HUMAN RESOURCE MANAGEMENT POLICIES AND ENTREPRENEURSHIP

Of all the managerial decision areas that can affect corporate entrepreneurship, human resource management (HRM) would seem to be one of the more vital. Indeed, the HRM field appears to be experiencing a fundamental transformation from a micro-oriented, bureaucracy-based, tool-driven discipline to one centered around the congruence of the various aspects of the HRM system with business strategies. The argument of Balkin and Logan (1988) that poorly designed compensation and performance appraisal systems may constrain entrepreneurial behavior in established firms is reflective of this transformation. Similarly, Schuler (1986) has suggested that organization-level entrepreneurship can be influenced by a large number of HRM-related policies.

The set of HRM policies and procedures available to managers includes numerous and varied choice alternatives. Schuler and Jackson (1987) have presented a typology of these alternatives that identifies key decision options in each of six areas: planning, staffing, appraising, compensating, training and development, and labor-management relations. Underlying the various decision options are a number of bipolar dimensions, such as the extent to which a given policy reflects an open versus closed, structured versus unstructured, or short-term versus long-term orientation. It would seem that particular organizational strategies, such as entrepreneurship, can be furthered by putting together consistent sets of HRM practices.

Entrepreneurial activities require employees to act and think in ways not normally associated with non-entrepreneurial or bureaucratic organizations. Based on his review of the literature, Schuler (1986) suggested the following employee characteristics were associated with successful entrepreneurial efforts: creative and innovative behavior, risk-taking, a long-term orientation, a focus on results, flexibility to change, cooperation, independent behavior, tolerance of ambiguity, and a preference to assume responsibility. He also notes that HRM practices are a reflection of a firm's culture, and others (Brandt, 1986; Cornwall and Perlman, 1990; Peters, 1987; Tropman and Morningstar, 1989) have suggested corporate entrepreneurship requires a culture built around emotional commitment, autonomy, empowerment, earned respect, and a strong work ethic. Using these desired employee and cultural characteristics, it becomes possible to identify the HRM policy combinations most conducive to fostering entrepreneurial behavior.

Let us now consider specific linkages. Beginning with job planning, innovation and risk-taking behaviors would seem more consistent with a long-term orientation and an emphasis on formal planning with high employee involvement. Job-related tasks would need to be broadly defined, with more decision-making discretion. Also, greater emphasis would have to be placed on results over process or procedure. Jobs are likely to be less structured or constrained by rigid organizational policies. Multiple policies and procedures, along with centralized decision making, tend to constrain action alternatives and inhibit the proactive decision-making necessary for successful entrepreneurial events.

Turning to the staffing choices of the firm, entrepreneurial behavior implies unpredictable external environments and internal requirements. The fit between company direction and available internal resources may be poor. Therefore, firms may be forced to rely on external sources for job candidates. The need to create and maintain an entrepreneurial culture, combined with a reliance on external sources of employees, would in turn increase the need for extensive orientation and socialization programs. Further, rapid environmental change and continuous product and market innovation can be expected to produce time pressures as well as variable job demands and requirements. The result in entrepreneurial organizations is likely to be a reliance on more general, more implicit, and less formalized selection criteria (Olian and Rynes, 1984; Roberts and Fusfeld, 1981).

Once a person is selected into the organization, staffing practices are likely to be designed around broad career paths and multiple ladders (Pearson, 1989). Broad paths and multiple ladders provide exposure to more areas of the organization and different ways of thinking. This exposure in turn enhances idea generation and problem solving and encourages cooperative activities. Staffing procedures in these organizations are apt to be fairly open. Entrepreneurial individuals are goal- and action-oriented. Thus, an employee should not be selected for, or assigned to, entrepreneurial tasks simply on the basis of past performance on other tasks or because they have the basic knowledge and skills the job requires. Open selection procedures allow for more self-selection into entrepreneurial positions and hence a better match between the entrepreneurial requirements of the organization and the individual's needs.

Training and development practices can promote entrepreneurial behavior to the extent that they are applicable to a broad range of job situations and encourage high employee participation. Changing job demands and the need to keep abreast of the newest technologies suggest a need for continuous, ongoing training, as well as training activities that are less structured or standardized and that focus on individualized knowledge requirements. This type of training approach enables employees to respond in unique ways to new challenges, adapt to dynamic environmental conditions, and feel comfortable with ambiguity. Training programs may also include an attitudinal component, wherein acceptance of change, a willingness to take risks and assume responsibility, and reliance on teamwork and shared achievements are central themes. Finally, it may be necessary to teach political skills to prospective entrepreneurs, including ways to obtain sponsors, build resource networks, and avoid early publicity of new concepts and ventures.

Organizations communicate performance expectations and reinforce desired employee behaviors through their performance appraisal and reward practices, both of which should be designed around specific criteria. Entrepreneurship can be fostered where performance evaluations and discretionary compensation are based on long-term results and a balance between individual and group performance (Balkin and Logan, 1988; Maidique, 1980; Morris, Avila and Allen, 1993). Moreover, given that risk implies failure, the appraisal and reward systems should reflect a tolerance of failure and offer some employment security. Because entrepreneurial individuals tend to demonstrate a high need for achievement but are also reward conscious, it is important that they be active participants both in setting high performance standards and in designing customized reward systems.

Appraisals should be conducted at intermittent and irregular time intervals in entrepreneurial organizations, rather than at uniform or fixed intervals. They should be tailored to the life cycle of a project. This is because entrepreneurial events require time to evolve, with each one encountering unique sets of obstacles and with various projects typically at different stages of development. In addition, entrepreneurial success often depends on the ability of employees to obtain resources from novel sources or in non-traditional ways and occasionally to violate or ignore standard company policies and procedures. Accordingly, performance appraisals will need to emphasize end results, or outcomes, rather than the methods employed to achieve those results. The evaluation of employees will need to include explicit measures of innovativeness and risk assumption, which implies some use of qualitative and subjective measures of performance (e.g., Jennings and Seaman, 1990).

With regard to rewards, personal incentives (financial and non-financial) are necessary to reinforce the risk-taking and persistence required to implement an entrepreneurial concept. To retain entrepreneurial employees, these incentives must be significant. Individual incentives must be balanced by rewards linked to group performance over periods of time longer than the typical semi-annual or annual review periods to encourage cooperative, interdependent behavior (Kanter, 1983; Reich, 1987; Stewart, 1989). Taking responsibility for innovation and achieving a long-term commitment can be furthered by compensation practices that emphasize external pay equity and incentives such as stock options and profit sharing. The customized nature of these reward systems also suggests that responsibility for their design and implementation be decentralized, or delegated to the divisional or departmental level. Table 7.3 represents a summary of HRM practices that are believed to be facilitators of entrepreneurship. This list is not intended to be comprehensive, but rather, captures a set of key strategic relationships based on the extant literature. Morris and Jones (1993) have provided some initial empirical evidence to support a number of the proposed relationships.

WHAT ABOUT PUBLIC SECTOR ORGANIZATIONS?

Entrepreneurship also has the same underlying dimensions when applied in a public sector context. Thus, entrepreneurial events can be characterized in terms

Table 7.3

Summary of the HRM Policies Proposed to Be Consistent with Entrepreneurial Behavior

General area	Practices encouraging entrepreneurship
Planning/overall job design	Reliance on formal planning Long-term orientation in planning and job design Implicit job analysis Jobs that are broad in scope Jobs with significant discretion Jobs that are less structured Integrative job design Results-oriented job design High employee involvement
Recruitment and selection	Reliance on external sources for candidates Broad career paths Multiple career ladders General, implicit, less formalized selection criteria Extensive job socialization Open recruitment and selective procedures
Training and development	Long-term career orientation Training with broad applications Individualized training High employee participation Unsystematic training Emphasis on managerial skills Continuous/ongoing training
Performance appraisal	High employee involvement Balanced individual-group orientation Emphasis on effectiveness over efficiency Results oriented (vs. process) Based on subjective criteria Emphasis on long-term performance Includes innovation and risk criteria Reflects tolerance of failure Appraisals based on project life cycle
Compensation/rewards	Emphasizes long-term performance Decentralized/customized at division or departmental levels Tailored to individuals Emphasizes individual performance with incentives for group efforts Merit and incentive-based Significant financial rewards Based on external equity

of their innovativeness, risk-taking, and proactiveness. Innovativeness will tend to be more concerned with novel process improvements, new services, and new organizational forms. Examples might include a drive-in window for voter registration, day care service for welfare mothers in job training programs, or a public/private joint venture to address AIDS awareness. Risk-taking involves pursuing initiatives that have a calculated likelihood of resulting in loss or failure. While public sector organizations cannot incur bankruptcy, failure can result in non-delivered services, cutbacks in service levels, programs or organizational unit closures, staff reassignments, and budget cuts. Although high visibility in the public sector typically means risk-taking is moderate to low, the public sector does undertake highly risky ventures, such as the controversial luggage handling system at the Denver, Colorado airport. There is also career-related risk in the public sector, for while it is difficult to fire people, advancement can be influenced by visible failures. Proactiveness entails an action-orientation, and an emphasis on anticipating and preventing public sector problems before they occur. This action-orientation includes creative interpretation of rules, skills at networking and leveraging of resources, and a high level of persistence and patience in effecting change.

Public sector entrepreneurship is much closer to entrepreneurship in a large corporation than to a new venture start-up. Both public and large private organizations typically have formalized hierarchies, established stakeholder groups with competing demands, deeply entrenched cultures, detailed rules and procedures to guide operations; a desire on the part of managers for power and security; and fairly rigid systems governing financial controls, cost allocations, budgeting, and employee rewards. Managers in both types of organizations are often more concerned with internal than external developments and tend to focus more on considerations of process than on outcomes. Public sector entrepreneurs, like those in large corporations, and unlike those in a start-up context, are not independent, do not "own" the innovations that they develop, and confront very finite limits on the rewards that they can receive; alternatively, they have more job security, are not personally assuming the financial risks associated with a project, and have access to an established pool of resources.

Arguments For and Against Public Sector Entrepreneurship

A number of arguments can be raised that challenge the role of entrepreneurial behavior in public sector organizations. Public employees are not in a position to put taxpayer monies at significant risk, and this combined with the difficulties in measuring risk-return trade-offs in the public sector usually makes high-risk pursuits inappropriate. In addition, high visibility and a need for consensus in decision making suggest that incremental change is more realistic than bold innovation. Also, the lengthy periods of time required for an entrepreneurial event to unfold are inconsistent with public sector budgeting and re-election cycles. Moreover, bureaucracy and the civil service system serve to protect the status quo, ostensibly from the arbitrary or politically influenced behavior of political leaders and public executives. As entrepreneurship is fundamentally about disrupting the status quo and affecting organizational change, again there would seem to be an inherent inconsistency.

At a more fundamental level, some would argue that entrepreneurship can result in innovative measures (e.g., user fees, redevelopment agencies, off-budget enterprises, investment revenues, tax-increment financing, and development fees) that enable public officials and public administrators to avoid voter approval and increase their autonomy, thereby undermining democracy. Further, entrepreneurship entails the pursuit of opportunity regardless of resources currently controlled, while public sector managers are often limited by legislative or regulatory statute to using only those resources formally assigned to their organizations. Finally, the mission, structure, and major initiatives of the public organization are dictated from outside sources (legislative bodies, councils, authorities). Public managers are expected to implement these dictates in a reasonably effective and efficient manner. Entrepreneurship, alternatively, represents an internal dynamic that can serve to change the strategic direction of an organization, potentially putting it in conflict with its stated mission or mandate. Similarly, entrepreneurial efforts can lead public enterprises to generate new services or fundraising schemes that effectively put them in competition with private sector enterprises, which the private sector might argue is a form of unfair competition.

The counter argument is that there have always been elements of innovation and entrepreneurship in public sector organizations, and that the issue is more one of formally defining the entrepreneurial role and then determining appropriate degrees and frequencies of entrepreneurship for a given organization, department, or unit. Creating value for customers, putting resources together in unique ways, and being opportunity-driven are not inherently in conflict with the mission or purpose of public agencies. This is why there does not appear to be any shortage of examples of successful innovations that originate in mainstream public organizations (e.g., Jordan, 1990; Moore, 1983).

There is, one could further suggest, a growing need for entrepreneurial approaches in public administration. The contemporary environment confronting public sector managers is far more complex, threatening, and dynamic than in years past. One has only to consider a public school. A few decades ago, the school was principally accountable for providing a sound, well-rounded basic education. Today, teachers and administrators are responsible for increasing computer literacy, deterring sexual harassment, detecting child abuse, discouraging drug consumption, ensuring the physical safety of students, facilitating bilingualism, providing aftercare, assisting those with learning disabilities, and accommodating those with physical handicaps. The ability to recognize and adequately respond to such changing circumstances is severely limited. Quite simply, the more turbulent the environment in which public managers must operate, the less effective is the traditional bureaucratic model.

Bureaucracy has many advantages and can be quite effective when operating in a relatively stable and predictable environment. However, when faced with highly turbulent environments where funding is not dependable, client demographics and needs are in flux, technology is rapidly changing, social and environmental pressures are increasing, skilled labor shortages are the norm, citizens are calling for privatization, litigation is rampant, and a host of other discontinuities continue to present themselves, the bureaucratic framework fails to provide the flexibility, adaptability, speed, or incentives for innovation that are critical for effectively carrying out the mission of the public enterprise.

There are, of course, different degrees of bureaucratization, and the higher the degree, the greater the conflict with entrepreneurship. Morris, Schindehutte, and Pitt (1996) review fourteen key characteristics of the highly bureaucratic organization that make it incompatible with higher levels of EI. This is not to suggest entrepreneurship as a comprehensive alternative to the bureaucratic model. However, it is proposed as a core component of any post-bureaucracy conceptualization of public sector management.

Bellone and Goerl (1992) agree that potential conflicts do exist between public entrepreneurship and democracy but suggest that these can be bridged with what they refer to as a "civic-regarding entrepreneurship." This conceptualization emphasizes accountability to the extent that the principles of democratic theory are incorporated into the design of entrepreneurial initiatives. In noting (p. 133) that "a strong theory of public entrepreneurship requires a strong theory of citizenship," they argue that such initiatives should be developed in ways that facilitate citizen education and participation. They cite as examples of ways to accomplish such participation, citizen budget committees, advisory boards, vehicles for elevating citizen choice (e.g., vouchers), and volunteerism.

Turning Obstacles into Facilitators

The distinct nature of the public sector operating environment creates significant obstacles to entrepreneurial behavior. While a number of these obstacles are the same as those faced by corporate entrepreneurs (e.g. elaborate control systems, long approval cycles, top-down management, closed communication channels, rules and procedures, fear of failure), some of them are unique to the public sector.

Ramamurti (1986) has identified six major barriers to entrepreneurship in the public sector work environment: multiplicity and ambiguity of goals (which is related to difficulties in defining one's customer); limited managerial autonomy and high potential interference; high visibility; skewed reward systems (i.e., penalizing failure); a short-term orientation (reinforced by budget and election cycles); and restrictive personnel policies (e.g., hiring, firing, promoting). To these we would add a lack of competitive incentives for improved performance, difficulties in segmenting or discriminating among users (i.e., services must be available to all), and a lack of accountability among managers for innovation and change.

Approached differently, however, obstacles such as these can be used to facilitate entrepreneurial behavior. For instance, Ramamurti (1986) proposes that goal ambiguity is a potential source of discretion to the entrepreneurial manager, that the media can be used as a source of power, and that outsiders can be co-opted to enable one to take organizational risks without taking personal risks.

There is no formal blueprint or model regarding how entrepreneurship can be accomplished in large established companies, and the same conclusion would seem to apply in the public sector. The key appears to be experimentation. While public sector managers do not have the luxury of being able to experiment freely with structures, control systems, rewards, communication systems, or budgeting methods, there is typically more room for flexibility than is acknowledged by so-called bureaucracy bashers. At the same time, and as noted earlier, the greatest obstacle to entrepreneurship is people themselves—managers and employees who fear failure and resist change. The individual who believes in his/her own ability to affect change, and who is in fact change oriented, will find ways around many of the other obstacles.

This brings us to the final question: Who is the public entrepreneur? Like their private sector counterparts, public sector entrepreneurs are not born. Work environments can be designed that accommodate the tendency to be entrepreneurial. Further, and in spite of the inherent obstacles, the public sector work environment may contain sufficient ambiguity, flexibility, and contradictions in values to leave room for the entrepreneur to operate.

Pinchot (1985) has done some interesting work attempting to conceptualize the corporate entrepreneur (which he calls the ''intrapreneur'') and contrast him/her with the start-up entrepreneur. In Figure 7.2 we have attempted to extend Pinchot's efforts to incorporate the public sector entrepreneur. The key characteristics being proposed include a mix of power and achievement motivation, an ability to work strategically—which depends on small steps, strong political and external networking skills, calculated risk-taking, and self-confidence—and an ability to tolerate and use ambiguity as a source of discretion.

CONCLUSIONS

Organizations tend to evolve through a number of stages while moving from relatively open and loosely structured start-up enterprises to large conglomerates with complex integrating mechanisms and extensive administrative bureaucracies. Along the way, the role of entrepreneurship changes, while the level of EI generally declines. For very logical reasons, managers put systems and structures in place that have the (usually unintended) side effect of constraining or discouraging entrepreneurial behavior.

In this chapter, we have provided a framework for identifying the obstacles or constraints on entrepreneurial intensity in organizations. They consist of systems, structures, strategic direction, policies and procedures, people and culture. This framework actually represents a blueprint for facilitating entrepreneurship if it is just turned upside down. That is, by doing such things as explicitly evaluating employees on innovative performance, creating slack in the control

Figure 7.2
Comparing Independent, Corporate, and Public Entrepreneurs

	Independent Entrepreneur	Corporate Entrepreneur	Public Sector Entrepreneur
PRIMARY MOTIVE	Wants freedom; goal oriented and self-reliant; achievement-motivated	Wants freedom and access to corporate resources; goal-oriented and self-motivated, but also responds to corporate rewards and recognition	Power motivated and achievement motivated; may think in grandiose terms; not constrained by profit motive
TIME ORIENTATION	End goals of 5-10 year growth of business	End goals of 3-15 years depending on type of venture	End goals of 10-15 years; begins with impressive short-term success, then implements long-term plan as series of short-term programs
SKILLS	Knows business intimately; more business acumen than managerial or political skill	Strong technical skills or product knowledge; good managerial skills; weak political skills	Strong political skills; able to develop power sources beyond those formally assigned; adept at using public relations and the media to advantage
ATTITUDE TOWARD SYSTEM	Frustrated by system so rejects it and starts his/her own	Dislikes system but learns to work within it and manipulate it	Tends to redesign or restructure the system to accomplish his/her own ends
FOCUS	External; markets and technology	Internal and external; builds internal networks and finds mentors or sponsors	Learns to co-opt or use external forces to accomplish internal change; builds constituencies of support among politicians, unions, the private sector, the media and the community
RISKS AND FAILURES	Assumes considerable financial and personal risk; identifies key risk factors and tries to minimize them; sees failure as learning experience	Likes moderate risks; principal risks are career-related, sensitive to need to appear orderly within corporation; hides risky projects so can learn from mistakes without political cost of public failure	Calculated risk-taker; takes big organizational risks without taking big personal risks by managing the process by which risky decisions are made; tends to deviate from rules only slightly at first, then progressively more; since failure is harder to define, will manage events to promote positive outcomes
COURAGE AND DESTINY	Self-confident, optimistic, bold	Self-confident, optimistic, bold; cynical about the system but believes he/she can manipulate it	Self-confident, optimistic, bold; high tolerance for ambiguity; uses ambiguity as a source of managerial discretion

Source: adapted from Pinchot (1985).

Figure 7.3
Integrating Entrepreneurship throughout the Organization

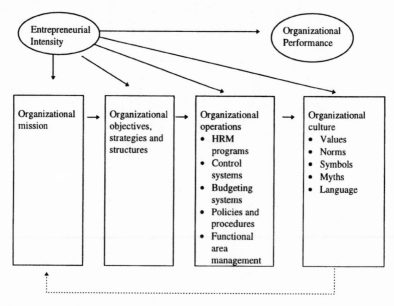

system, flattening the organizational structure, broadening spans of control, setting innovation objectives, shortening approval cycles, removing documentation requirements, and reducing the perceived costs of failure, management can create entrepreneurial work environments.

In the final analysis, EI represents an attitudinal and behavioral orientation that should pervade all aspects of an organization. As demonstrated in Figure 7.3, there is a direct positive link between EI and company performance. Further, the effectiveness of this linkage depends on how well integrated entrepreneurship is into the mission, objectives, strategies, structures, operations, and culture of the enterprise. The basic responsibility of management becomes one of determining the appropriate degree and amount of EI for the organization overall, and for each major functional area within the organization's operations.

REFERENCES

Adizes, I. 1978. "Organizational Passages—Diagnosing and Treating Lifecycle Problems of Organizations." *Organizational Dynamics* (Summer), 2–25.

Balkin, D.B., and Logan, J.W. 1988. "Reward Policies that Support Entrepreneurship." *Compensation and Benefits Review*, 20, 18–25.

Bellone, Carl J., and George, F.G. 1992. "Reconciling Public Entrepreneurship and Democracy." *Public Administration Review*, 52 (2) (March–April), 130–134.

Bird, B.J. 1989. *Entrepreneurial Behavior*. Glenview, IL: Scott, Foresman and Co.

Brandt, S.C. 1986. *Entrepreneuring in Established Companies*. Homewood, IL: Dow Jones–Irwin.

Cornwall, J.R., and Perlman, B. 1990. *Organizational Entrepreneurship*. Homewood, IL: Irwin Publishing.

Griener, L.E. 1972. "Evolution and Revolution as Organizations Grow." *Harvard Business Review* (July–August), 37–46.

Jennings, D.F., and Lumpkin, J.R. 1989. "Functional Modeling Corporate Entrepreneurship: An Empirical Integrative Analysis." *Journal of Management*, 15 (2), 485–502.

Jennings, D.F., and Seaman, S.L. 1990. "Aggressiveness of Response to New Business Opportunities Following Deregulation: An Empirical Study of Established Financial Firms." *Journal of Business Venturing*, 5 (October), 177–189.

Jordan, F. 1990. *Innovating America*. New York: The Ford Foundation.

Kanter, R.M. 1983. *The Change Masters*. New York: Simon & Schuster.

Kao, J. 1989. *Entrepreneurship, Creativity and Organization*. Englewood Cliffs, NJ: Prentice-Hall.

Kerr, S. 1975. "On the Folly of Rewarding A, While Hoping for B." *Academy of Management Journal*, 18 (December), 769–783.

Knight, R.M. 1987. "Corporate Innovation and Entrepreneurship: A Canadian Study." *Journal of Product Innovation Management*, 4 (4), 284–297.

Maidique, M.A. 1980. "Entrepreneurs, Champions and Technological Innovation." *Sloan Management Review*, 21, 59–76.

Miller, D., and Friesen, P.H. 1983. "Strategy-Making and Environment: The Third Link." *Strategic Management Journal*, 4, 221–235.

Moore, B.H. (ed.) 1983. *The Entrepreneur in Local Government*. Washington, DC: International City Management Association.

Morris, M.H., Avila, R., and Allen, J. 1993. "Individualism and the Modern Corporation: Implications for Innovations and Entrepreneurship." *Journal of Management*, 19, 3.

Morris, H.H., and Jones, F. 1993. "Human Resource Management Practices and Corporate Entrepreneurship: An Empirical Assessment." *International Journal of Human Resources Management*, 4 (3), 28–43.

Morris, M.H., Schindehutte, M., and Pitt, L.F. 1996. "Sustaining the Entrepreneurial Society." *Small Business Foundation of America: The Research Institute for Emerging Enterprise*. Working Paper, 1 (March).

Morris, M.H., and Sexton, D.L. 1996. "The Concept of Entrepreneurial Intensity: Implications for Company Performance." *Journal of Business Research*, 36 (1), 5–14.

Olian, J.D. and Rynes, S.L. 1984. "Organizational Staffing: Integrating Practice with Strategy." *Industrial Relations*, 23, 170–183.

Pearson, G.J. 1989. "Promoting Entrepreneurship in Large Companies." *Long Range Planning*, 22 (3), 87–97.

Peters, T.J. 1987. *Thriving on Chaos*. New York: Alfred A. Knopf.

Pinchot, G. 1985. *Intrapreneuring*. New York: Harper and Row.

Ramamurti, R. 1986. "Public Entrepreneurs: Who They Are and How They Operate." *California Management Review*, 28 (3) (Spring), 142–158.

Reich, R. 1987. "Entrepreneurship Reconsidered: The Team as Hero." *Harvard Business Review*, 65 (May–June), 77–83.

Roberts, E.B., and Fusfeld, A.R. 1981. "Staffing the Innovative Technology Based Organization." *Sloan Management Review* (Spring), 19–34.

Schuler, R.S. 1986. "Entrepreneurship in Organizations." *Human Resource Management* (Winter), 614–629.

Schuler, R.S., and Jackson, S.E. 1987. "Linking Competitive Strategies with Human Resource Management Practices." *Academy of Management Executive*, 1, 207–219.

Souder, W. 1987. *Managing New Product Innovations*. Lexington, MA: D.C. Heath & Co.

Stefflre, V. 1985. "Organizational Obstacles to Innovation: A Formulation of the Problem." *Journal of Product Innovation Management*, 2, 3–11.

Stevenson, H., Roberts, M.J., and Grousbeck, H.I. 1994. *New Business Ventures and the Entrepreneur*, 4th ed. Burr Ridge, IL: Irwin.

Stewart, A. 1989. *Team Entrepreneurship*. Newbury Park, CA: Sage.

Tropman, J.E., and Morningstar, G. 1989. *Entrepreneurial Systems for the 1990's*. New York: Quorum Books.

Zeithaml, C.D., and Zeithaml, V.A. 1984. "Environmental Management: Revising the Marketing Perspective." *Journal of Marketing*, 18 (Spring).

8

Entrepreneurship at the Societal Level

INTRODUCTION

As the millennium draws to a close, the world is witnessing an unprecedented movement toward free enterprise. The end of the Cold War, the passing of Soviet client state linkages, and the market reforms that the International Monetary Fund and the World Bank impose with increasing vigor on financially wayward nations contribute to this movement. The emergence of the North American, South American, European Community, and Pacific Rim trading blocks is testimony to a multilateral desire to radically reduce trade barriers. The General Agreement on Tariffs and Trade (GATT) agreements are an expression of this goal worldwide.

Such developments are much more than a sign that the West won the Cold War. Even in traditionally capitalistic countries, fundamental questions are being raised about the nature and scope of government's role in the economy and in facilitating societal quality of life. Hence, one finds that the public agenda has shifted toward consideration of such issues as privatization, devolution of federal power, voucher programs, tax reductions, and restructuring of taxation systems. Recognition is growing that markets work and that they work best when left to their own devices.

And yet, it is not enough to simply install or enhance market mechanisms. Entrepreneurship is the engine that drives market-based economies. It is the entrepreneurial individual or team that identifies and capitalizes on opportunity, puts together unique combinations of resources, assumes risks, and manages and harvests a venture. The problem, then, becomes one of not simply encouraging competition, the profit motive, the price mechanism, private property, and the freely interacting forces of supply and demand, but one of creating infrastructures and facilitating environments conducive to entrepreneurial behavior.

THREE EXAMPLES OF ENTREPRENEURIAL ECONOMIES

Nations vary in terms of their levels of entrepreneurial intensity (EI). Some are good at breakthrough innovation, others at imitation. Ultimately, though, the question is one of how dynamic and growth-oriented the country is. Unfortunately, there currently is no measure available of EI at a national level. One could look at new business start-up rates, patents issued, new product announcements, or other such indicators, but the availability of reliable data is inconsistent across nations. Nonetheless, it is possible to identify countries that have achieved high rates of sustained growth and that continue to demonstrate a strong growth orientation.

Three such countries are Singapore, South Korea, and Chile. Each is a modern, or relatively recent, success story. Each has moved from being a poor third-world debtor nation to having economies that are rapidly growing and that have produced dramatic improvements in per capita gross domestic product (GDP). Their paths to success have been different, with one emphasizing the attraction of multinationals and the development of a domestic technological base, another stressing the development of capital-intensive industry with a strong export focus, and the third concentrating on fiscal conservatism and the unleashing of free market capitalism internally. Government has played critical, but very different, roles in each case. In all three countries, however, the ultimate focus has been to create domestic environments that are conducive to entrepreneurial behavior on the part of individuals and organizations.

Let us briefly look at each of these case studies.

Singapore

Singapore is one of the great success stories of the twentieth century. Since achieving autonomy (1959) and independence (1965), it has achieved remarkable growth, especially in the post–1980 period. It has evolved from an economy based on plentiful low-cost labor (i.e., a factor-driven economy) to one that is investment-driven and innovation-driven. It is an important secondary home base to multinationals, while boasting a growing number of successful indigenous companies.

Tang and Yeo (1995) compare the national development of Singapore to the development of an entrepreneurial firm. They argue that "technopreneurship," or the mix of technological competence and entrepreneurship, has played a key role in Singapore's progress. According to these authors, Singapore has evolved through three stages: start-up, competence building, and selective pioneering. At start-up, the nation had limited resources and technological competence and had to leverage resources (expertise, finance) by attracting multinationals. Government played a leadership role in building infrastructures, developing human resources, and gaining the confidence of investors with innovative and pragmatic policies. In stage two, and now with a sufficient quantity of technically-qualified members of the workforce, two things occurred. The government convinced multinational investors to increase levels of investment to cover more sophisticated means of production and emphasize high-value-added, upstream activities and products. At the same time, local entrepreneurs and indigenous companies began to enter into technology businesses on a notable scale. The government instituted policies that encouraged a symbiotic relationship between foreign multinationals and growing local companies. In stage three, Singapore began to target selective technological fields in which it could be among the world's leaders. The government helps detect trends but defers to the private sector in actually pioneering new ventures. The focus is on initiatives with the least controlled uncertainty, and especially the development or adoption of new and emerging technologies. By now, lower-end production operations have been relocated to lower-cost countries.

In Singapore, this evolution occurred because of what Tang and Yeo (1995) call "government entrepreneurship." The government has developed strategic policies and programs and then demonstrated consistency and perseverance in following the planned course of action. It has been opportunity-oriented, detecting and moving on new opportunities as they arose. Daring investments have been made when they had to be. Most importantly, the government created an infrastructure and environment that helped entrepreneurs prepare themselves, get on their feet, and grow, but then the government got out of their way.

South Korea

South Korea is also a story of dramatic turnaround and success. Constrained during this century by 35 years of repressive colonization by Japan, and a devastating civil war that resulted in the partitioning of North Korea from the south, the country has experienced dramatic economic growth over the past three decades. Average incomes have risen from $100 to $8,500 per year, while annual growth has averaged between 5 and 10% in real terms (Mallaby, 1995).

The so-called Korean model of economic development is a growth-obsessed model. While there is some debate as to the exact nature of this model, it can be characterized by a strong export orientation (including the need to meet international standards), an emphasis on heavy manufacturing, and a mix of private enterprise, competition, educational investment, and stable macroeconomic policy. Just as important, though, were draconian labor policies, the squeezing of savers (with negative real returns) to spur investment, political repression, and the achievement of growth by sacrifice. Building on a well-educated labor force in the 1960's, the government both subsidized and coordinated investment decisions. Export industries were pushed, and the government directed companies on what to produce, what to charge, and how much to borrow. All of this was complemented by an internal investment boom, with significant demand for imported capital goods.

However, growth from squeezing more and more savings and labor out of the citizenry is not sustainable. Further, the government maintained a heavy hand in far too many facets of the economy long after it was necessary, while its policies have resulted in the domination of the economy by relatively inefficient "chaebol" (e.g., Hyundai, Daewoo, Samsung), or large industry groups.

A major backlash by workers and the public at large led to significant democratic reforms beginning in the late 1980's. Also, various policies have attempted to rein in the power of the "chaebol," subsidies to major industries have been cut, and companies are now freer to make their own strategic decisions. And, while the "chaebol" remain dominant and there is much more to be done in terms of meaningful deregulation, South Korea has maintained its amazing growth rate. Much of this is due to the momentum from years of sacrifice, but perhaps more critical is a culture that emphasizes an external focus, learning, flexibility, and aggressiveness.

Chile

A third example of a more entrepreneurial economy is Chile, easily the star performer of South America in recent decades. Relatively low inflation, high foreign reserves, government budget surpluses, low unemployment, a stable institutional investment base, and significant foreign investment (over $1 billion per year in recent years) all characterize Chile today. Annual growth in GDP has exceeded 6% since 1985.

If there is a "Chilean model," its three tenets are macro-economic stability, a vigorous private sector, and a liberal export-oriented trading environment ("The Miracle Unmasked," 1995). At the root of it all is a 25-year period of experimentation with radical free market initiatives. Tight fiscal and monetary policies, privatization, elimination of trade barriers, deregulation of the labor market, a private pension system (in which nearly the entire working population was enrolled in private pension fund management companies), and a general reduction in the size of government have been pursued aggressively. Importantly, structural reform followed macroeconomic stabilization, as the latter proved to be a prerequisite for the success of the former (Bosworth et al., 1994).

Chile also witnessed a transfer to democratic government in 1990. Both the military government under Pinochet and the subsequent democratic government have been less susceptible to the influence of pressure groups and lobbies. While the new leadership has invested in social programs and much-needed infrastructure, they have generally stuck to a course of economic liberalization. For example, capital controls have been partially loosened in recent years. Alternatively, the indexing of prices continues to be a problem that works against further reductions in inflation.

Although the Chilean economy boasts a number of large enterprises, most notably in copper and mining, small and medium-size firms play a major role in producing growth (Pilling, 1994). The strategic focus in Chile today continues to be on export businesses, which account for nearly two-thirds of GDP, on achieving more diversity in the export base, on major infrastructural investment, and on social upliftment (Beerman, 1996).

SUSTAINING THE ENTREPRENEURIAL SOCIETY: THE RULES OF THE GAME

It becomes clear from these examples that, even at the societal level, entrepreneurship is a manageable phenomenon. If entrepreneurship were viewed as a societal resource, with each country having a rich potential reserve of this resource, then societal-level efforts should address two questions:

1. How can this resource be most effectively allocated?
2. Are there things we can do to grow the amount of this resource residing within the people and organizations that make up the society?

These are not independent questions, as entrepreneurship can be allocated in ways that actually serve to increase the amount of entrepreneurship. Consider, for instance, a change in regulation involving the creation or removal of rules so as to permit or incentivize the establishment of innovative financing sources, such as venture capital firms (of which some countries have few or none). This rule change is, in effect, a decision to reallocate society's entrepreneurial resources towards more high-risk activities (given the typical investment profile of a venture capital firm compared, say, to a commercial bank). When those with financial resources take advantage of the rule change or incentive and set up a venture capital firm, this development represents an entrepreneurial event. This event in turn makes it possible for other individuals to get funding they otherwise might go without. They then start firms with innovative new products and services, which also represent entrepreneurial events. Each of these firms then serves as a training ground within which some employees learn how entrepreneurship works, only to subsequently break away and start their own ventures.

The allocation issue is also more than a question of whether people choose to do or not to do entrepreneurial things. Just as important is what they do. Decisions to commercialize a product invention, introduce a new method of production, open a new market for an existing product, implement a new franchising approach, or tap a new source of supply represent alternative courses of action that are more or less attractive depending on society's rewards and sanctions. Baumol (1990) makes a convincing case that other (what he terms "unproductive") options exist for the channeling of entrepreneurial energies, such as the discovery of a previously unused legal gambit that is effective in diverting returns to those who are first in exploiting it.

The rules determine the perceived costs and benefits of different types of entrepreneurial activity. Thus one could argue that the lucrative drug or automobile highjacking trades in an urban ghetto represent a very logical channeling of entrepreneurial energy given the opportunity costs. Both the upside and downside potentials of such activities are a function of the rules of the game that define opportunities, or the lack thereof, open to ghetto youth. Examples of "unproductive" entrepreneurship such as these, or the legal gambit mentioned above, have led Baumol (1990) to conclude that the net level of innovativeness and growth in society is strongly affected by the extent to which society's rules and rewards result in more value being placed on productive versus unproductive entrepreneurial behavior.

The rules and rewards of the game are many, as we shall see in the next chapter. They range from tax structures and health and safety regulation to the treatment of bankruptcy, intellectual property protection, licensing rules, and antitrust legislation. These rules also serve to reflect and reinforce the social and cultural values of society, such as whether those who succeed in commercial enterprise are held in higher or lower esteem than, say, those who succeed in politics, the arts, the military, or academe.

Sustainable entrepreneurship at the societal level is also a matter of the model used in writing the rules of the game. One model involves trying to identify the people and organizations in society with more entrepreneurial potential and then targeting society's resources to those individuals. This is what can be termed the "picking the winners" approach and is analogous to a banker deciding who does and does not receive a business loan. A second model concentrates on creating a supportive environment that allows entrepreneurial people and organizations to self-identify themselves and "step up to the plate." The second model, which we can label the "building the infrastructure" approach, assumes that environments can be created that help people and organizations develop their own entrepreneurial potential over time. It could be argued that the South Korean model was, at least initially, closer to "picking the winners," while the Chilean example is reflective of "building the infrastructure." As a generalization, we believe the "building the infrastructure" model is much more conducive to sustainable entrepreneurship (see also Davidsson, 1992).

THE IMPLICATIONS OF SOCIETAL ENTREPRENEURSHIP: IMPACT ON QUALITY OF LIFE

We have addressed the ideas that some countries can be more entrepreneurial than others, and that countries can improve their own levels of entrepreneurship. One might conclude from this discussion that a fundamental value judgement is being made: namely that, all other things being equal, more entrepreneurship is better than less at the societal level. But is it? What are the implications of higher levels of entrepreneurship for societal well-being or quality of life (QOL)? Clearly, where countries have experienced dramatic growth in a relatively short period of time, such as in South Korea, there is a quality of life price to be paid. But even in more stable economies, such as the United States, entrepreneurship has both short-term and long-term impacts on QOL.

Although there are as many definitions of societal QOL as there are people, issues such as "well-being" and "life satisfaction" are discussed by most who have studied the topic. For example, Sirgy et al. (1985) described societal QOL as a composite of both psychological (i.e., life satisfaction) and physical (i.e., life expectancy) well-being. Granzin (1987) suggests that perceived QOL is a function of the degree of satisfaction that one finds in a certain state of affairs as compared with a desired state of affairs. In addition, QOL has been approached using need satisfaction theories (e.g., those of Maslow, 1970). For instance, Sirgy et al. (1985) discusses improvements in QOL as a movement from satisfaction of lower-order needs (i.e., physiological needs, safety needs) towards higher-order needs (i.e., self-actualization).

For our purposes, societal QOL can be defined as the general state of well-being experienced by society's members. It is comprised of both objective (material conditions of life) and subjective (perceptions or evaluations of well-being) components (Campbell, 1976). While these components appear distinct, they are, in fact, very closely interrelated (Withey, 1972).

Although the overall concern is society's general well-being, the specific dimensions that constitute societal QOL are less apparent. The totality of life has been defined by Rice et al. (1985, p. 296) as a "mosaic field consisting of many specific domains of life in which an individual participates." Many observers have attempted to define specific domains, but no consensus has been reached. Day (1987) provided a summary listing of thirteen life-experience domains. However, his focus was at the level of the individual. When applied at a societal level, these experiences can be collapsed into seven domains:

Economic. the general state of the economy as reflected by economic vitality, economic stability, the position of the economy within the world economy, and the availability and quality of goods and services.

Health. the general state of mental and physical well-being of the society and the quality and availability of medical products, services, and facilities.

Social. the general state of security, values, attitudes, lifestyles, and norms as related to human development and need satisfaction.

Technological. the general state of effectiveness/efficiency of techniques and processes for converting resource inputs to goods and services.

Work. the general state of well-being in the work/organizational environment in terms of such issues as job satisfaction, job security, and job safety.

Institutional. the general state of societal institutions such as governmental (national security, welfare services, taxes, etc.), educational, religious, business, and family units in terms of their ability to meet societal needs.

Ecological. the general state of the natural environment in terms of such issues as resource preservation and conservation.

These domains are reasonably comprehensive, given their broad definitions, but not mutually exclusive. To assess the net impact of entrepreneurship on societal QOL, we must draw implications for each.

Impact of Entrepreneurship on Societal QOL

Whereas entrepreneurship produces a variety of both functional and dysfunctional effects in each of the domains, some of the more salient implications are summarized in Table 8.1. Each is discussed in more detail below.

Economic

Entrepreneurship increases economic vitality through the creation of new products and services. Additional jobs are generated to support the production and delivery of these goods and services. For instance, it is estimated that 80% of new jobs created in the past two decades resulted from entrepreneurial efforts (e.g., Birch, 1981). The economic activity that results from these new products and additional jobs results in greater overall societal wealth and a higher standard of living.

Schumpeter (1950) has suggested that entrepreneurship, not price competition, is the driving force behind development in market economies. Specifically, entrepreneurs produce the dynamic innovations that keep the capitalist engine in motion. These innovations serve to continually revolutionize the economy, at the same time making existing products and methods obsolete. Hence, entrepreneurs are involved in a process of "creative destruction." Foster (1986) has echoed this argument in claiming that successful companies are those willing to replace profitable product lines with potentially more profitable lines.

There is an alternative perspective that emphasizes negative economic outcomes resulting from entrepreneurship. Critics argue that increases in wealth resulting from entrepreneurial efforts are at an individual level and of little benefit to the aggregate economy. Optimization of wealth at an individual level may be suboptimal for society. Marx (in Tucker, 1978) went further, in arguing that entrepreneurship is predicated on private property, individualism, and greed, and that entrepreneurs are in an endless race with one another to "accumulate or be accumulated." They exploit the surplus value of labor in the form of profits, pay artificially low wages, and are forced over time to replace labor with capital.

In addition, entrepreneurship has been criticized for its reliance on high-risk resource utilization, as evidenced in the high rate of new product and service failures. As a result, entrepreneurship has the potential to magnify the peaks and troughs of business cycle activity. Discontinuous innovation not only makes existing products and processes obsolete but generates significant investment as other firms seek to imitate the innovations. Expectations can be raised beyond

Table 8.1
Positive and Negative Effects of Entrepreneurship on Societal QOL

QOL Dimensions	Effects of Entrepreneurship	
	Functional	Dysfunctional
Economic	Greater economic vitality via increases in GDP and the creation of jobs Increased societal wealth and higher standards of living	Creation of individual wealth versus societal wealth Higher risk use of resources More pronounced cyclical swings in the economy Loss in the competitive position of large established firms
Health	Medical product, service, and process innovations	Greater stress levels as a result of greater incidence of change
Social	Improvements in material affluence leading to increased emphasis on the higher-order needs of society Greater societal confidence in the state of progress and security	Disruptions of existing attitudes and lifestyles Unethical and/or immoral business behaviors in an attempt to quickly capitalize on profit opportunities becomes an acceptable standard
Technological	Proactive, cutting edge technological innovations and transfers Greater resource productivity as a result of improved production techniques Improved competitive position within a global business environment	Acceleration of technology life cycles resulting in higher product and business failure rate Dynamic, unpredictable, competitive environment Disruptive technostructural organizational change
Work life	Organizational behavioral benefits due to entrepreneurial cultures Superior organizational performance due to improved productivity, quality, and the development of new products, services, and processes	Job dissatisfaction on the part of employees with high resistance both to idiosyncratic behavior of the entrepreneurial personality and to organizational change Rapid obsolescence of employee work skills Greater emphasis on individual rather than group or division
Institutional	Increased tax base and lower costs of government services Increased opportunities and greater ability to meet consumer/societal needs	Challenges to the structure, roles, and missions of many societal institutions Need for new rules and procedures which complicate administrative processes Anti-managerial biases may develop
Ecological	Creative solutions to resource scarcity and environmental crises	Wasted resources as a result of unneeded innovation and rapid product obsolescence Depleted resources due to rapid economic growth Damage to natural environment from unfettered economic growth

the levels justified by the nature of the innovation, ultimately resulting in over-production and recession.

Further, as the criticism of Ferguson (1988) and Reich (1987) illustrate, an economic system that facilitates small entrepreneurial companies at the expense of large established firms may weaken the global competitiveness of a nation by fragmenting industries. Entrepreneurs capitalize on the huge investments and technological developments of established firms to create profitable ventures. However, in an attempt to remain competitive, they undermine the larger firms and society as a whole by selling the technology (or themselves) to the highest bidder—often an offshore competitor. Moreover, entrepreneurial firms stress breakthrough innovations to the exception of more incremental product and process improvements necessary for companies to sustain a competitive edge over time.

Health

Entrepreneurial societies produce high rates of innovation in medical proc-esses, products, and services, which leads to greater physical and mental well-being for most societal groups. Many historically terminal diseases now have cures or treatments, and there is optimism that most disease will one day be remedied. The development of advanced pharmaceutical and medical products has extended average life spans and reduced physical suffering in most societies.

On the dysfunctional side, entrepreneurship often leads to greater levels of stress for those affected by the significant and sometimes dramatic change that results from the entrepreneurial process. Current medical beliefs suggest that stress is associated with a substantial portion of all physical and mental illnesses. In addition, an inability to cope with the societal pressures that accompany entrepreneurial change can result in heightened levels of alcoholism and drug abuse.

Social

In societies where the functional aspects of entrepreneurship are evident, ma-terial affluence leads to the satisfaction of lower-order needs (i.e., physiological and security). As a result, societal goals can be focused on the fulfilment of higher-order needs. In addition, confidence in the state of societal progress and security may improve as a result of entrepreneurial advancements. The end result is that human development is enhanced.

At the same time, entrepreneurship can lead to the disruption of societal at-titudes, norms, and lifestyles. New products and services have the potential not only to speed the pace of life but also to change the way it is lived. An example is the development over the past 25 years of a "disposable society" in the United States. In addition, new innovations can create ethical dilemmas, such as medical advances that have the ability to perpetuate human life for longer and longer time periods.

A different perspective was provided by Veblen (1967), who criticized entrepreneurs for purposely disrupting or undermining the established social order and reaping profits from the resulting confusion. In his view, entrepreneurs are saboteurs who create chaos for self-gain.

The preoccupation of some entrepreneurs with immediate profits also has dysfunctional social implications. Unbridled entrepreneurship can lead to a preoccupation with doing whatever is necessary to achieve success. The entrepreneur's obsession with making it happen, combined with the primacy placed on individualism and independence and a disdain for the rules and constraints of societal institutions, can encourage more than rule-bending. Tacitly unethical or illegal behavior is sometimes a by-product, and where the entrepreneur is held in high esteem, society may come to believe that such behavior is acceptable. Similarly, the entrepreneurial quest for material gain may produce a societal focus on materialism.

Technological

Entrepreneurship is a major factor behind the increased pace of technological progress today. Entrepreneurs have been responsible for both technological innovations (the development of new processes and methods) and technological transfers (the application of new processes and methods to the development and delivery of products and services). Also, where resources are scarce, entrepreneurial efforts that result in new production techniques can lead to greater productivity per resource unit. As a consequence, successful entrepreneurial efforts result in greater satisfaction of consumer needs via the efficient production of more high quality products and services.

In addition, through major technological advances, a society can significantly enhance its competitive position within world markets. As Young (1985) has noted, successful challenges to the dominant global competitive position of the United States can be substantially attributed to inadequate investment in the development and application of new technologies. Drucker (1985) concludes that no country can have a viable high-tech sector without having an entrepreneurial economy.

Yet, rapid technological advancements give rise to greater environmental turbulence and complexity. As entrepreneurship spawns new and better technologies for delivering products and services, a higher rate of business failure is likely to occur. Functionally useful products are made obsolete. The competitive arena for the organizations affected becomes more dynamic and less predictable. Technological forecasting becomes critical. Firms are forced to implement technostructural changes that may be highly disruptive to the operations of the organization in the short-term, and sometimes permanently.

Work

Quality of work life is affected in a variety of ways by entrepreneurship. Firms that encourage and support entrepreneurial efforts typically develop cultures that focus on identifying, and capitalizing on, new opportunities. Employees find ample rewards for innovative and creative ideas that facilitate the exploitation of such opportunities. Employee independence is encouraged; flat management structures with multiple informal networks typically prevail. Employees retain greater individual freedom to make the decisions necessary to accomplish their work goals. Where employees appreciate and desire relative independence, significant organizational behavioral benefits can occur. Higher productivity, improved quality, and a faster rate of new product and service introduction are the end result.

Such freedoms are not always perceived as positive, however. As many industries have matured, associated organizations have evolved into relatively bureaucratic institutions with well-defined work rules and procedures. Employees of organizations such as these have become comfortable with the level of predictability and stability in their work routine. For such employees, the challenges of being involved in a truly entrepreneurial firm may not be appealing.

Entrepreneurs create change, make new rules, demand resource support, and set new standards of performance. Their charisma, while inspiring, may also be perceived as threatening. Further, entrepreneurial managers can alienate subordinates with behaviors that reflect their personal need for control, sense of distrust, need for applause, and overall defensiveness (Kets de Vries, 1984). Employees can also find that the organizational changes brought about by the entrepreneurial process lead to rapid obsolescence of work skills. For individual employees who feel secure in stable and predictable work environments, the organizational instabilities that result from entrepreneurial efforts can lead to deteriorating job satisfaction and job security.

Reich (1987) posited that entrepreneurship suffers from a preoccupation with the individual. The entrepreneur is glorified, whereas the critical others who contribute to his/her success are assumed to be replaceable. As a result, entrepreneurship tends to produce major new breakthroughs and cutting-edge scientific discoveries but not the incremental improvements and cost reductions that result from collective action over time. Reich suggested that the latter type of progress can best be achieved by an emphasis on collective entrepreneurship or the "team as hero."

Institutional

In any society, institutions (e.g., governmental, educational, religious) exist to serve specific needs of the aggregate population. Institutional QOL is improved to the extent that entrepreneurship has a positive effect on the functioning of such institutions. For example, entrepreneurial ventures create an enhanced tax base that can be used by governmental bodies to support social services. Further, entrepreneurial attempts at privatization have the potential to reduce the cost of many government functions. Innovations in technology make it possible to provide more universal educational opportunities, including opportunities for the economically disadvantaged and the handicapped. Religious institutions find that they are able to communicate and tailor their services to larger numbers of people. Businesses are able to employ more people and produce a wider array of goods and services.

At the same time, entrepreneurial efforts challenge the structure, mission, and roles of many institutions. For instance, advances in medical technology have created challenges to the role of organized religion in family planning, while opportunities for female entrepreneurship have challenged the role and functioning of the family unit. Unions have found their power undermined by the rapid growth in entrepreneurial start-up ventures. Moreover, the need for new rules and procedures to facilitate entrepreneurship complicates the administrative processes in established institutions and may lead to ineffective performance.

In a related vein, Kaplan (1987) claimed that entrepreneurship produces an anti-managerial bias, wherein large firms and corporate managers are denigrated. He believes that entrepreneurship would not be possible in modern society without the stability provided by huge private conglomerates, public utilities, and charitable institutions.

Ecological

Environmentalists speak of ecological problems that will eventually invade the daily lives of people in all societies. Concerns are voiced about population crises, pollution crises, resource scarcities, and related problems that form the basis of the limited growth thesis. And yet, where entrepreneurship has led to more rapid increases in production than in consumption, the arguments of the limited growth proponents are weakened. Entrepreneurial ideas have spurred important and unique mechanisms for conserving, and in some cases, creating additional resources. For example, Enis (1987) discussed the impact of the development of a heavy manufacturing industry in outer space on the ecological position of this planet. Innovations have permitted more to be produced with less, eliminated sources of pollution, and replaced natural resources with synthetic substitutes.

In contrast, entrepreneurship can aggravate ecological problems when failed ideas and efforts lead to wasted resources. Even entrepreneurial successes can lead to wasted resources when new products and services cause perfectly functional goods and services to become obsolete. Additionally, the fast pace of economic growth resulting from entrepreneurial efforts can lead to rapid depletion of societal resources. Where entrepreneurship is intense, growth becomes more uncontrolled, and the assets of the environment can be damaged and destroyed.

QUALITY OF LIFE, GROWTH, AND THE
ENTREPRENEURIAL DYNAMIC

Entrepreneurship has a significant long-term impact on all QOL dimensions (see Table 8.2). This impact is greatest on the economic dimension. While there is little conclusive evidence, economic QOL would seem to account for a larger proportion of total QOL than does any other dimension (e.g., Pennings, 1982). For instance, an economically prosperous society is more able to develop technology or improve work conditions.

Entrepreneurship is fundamentally a celebration of growth. But growth has been a source of considerable controversy over the centuries. In contemporary times, a no-growth school argues that continued growth has only resulted in a population explosion and consequent malnutrition, depletion of critical natural resources, pollution and its ill effects on the environment and on personal health, an ethic of materialism and greed, and modernism (e.g., Schumacher, 1973; Meadows et al., 1972). Growth critics predict that the future will bring the exponential growth of population and capital, followed by social and economic collapse, as well as a stop to industrial growth, exacerbated levels of economic inequality, and a dismal, depleted existence. Proposed solutions have included deliberate restrictions on growth, learning to live with less, redistribution of income, and a radical transformation of moral values.

The response from growth proponents emphasizes that QOL is better today for more people than at any time in history, that the projective facts and meth-

Table 8.2
Net Impacts of Entrepreneurial Intensity on QOL

Major QOL Domain*	Dominant Impact of Entrepreneurship	Net Impact
E, W	Extensive Job Creation	Positive
E	Sizable Income/Wealth Creation	Positive
E, H, T	Most New Innovation	Positive
E, T, Ec	Rapid Product Obsolescence	Negative
Ec	More Efficient Resource Utilization	Positive
Ec	Rapid Depletion of Existing Resources	Negative
Ec	High-Risk Use of Resources	Negative
W	Greater Opportunities for Employee Development/Advancement	Positive
W, I	Less Concern for Family Relationships	Negative
S, Ec	Pressure for Expediency/Unethical Behavior	Negative
H, W, I	High Levels of Personal Stress	Negative
I	More Personal Freedom	Positive

*Key: E = Economic, H = Health, S = Social, T = Technological, W = Work Life, I = Institutional, EC = Ecological.

odologies used by the growth critics are fundamentally flawed, and that although real and severe problems exist, human ingenuity will produce creative solutions. They cite doomsayers of the past whose predictions were proven wrong because of technological change, and they note more recent research indicating some of the resource and environmental problems are less severe than previously thought or are not as directly related to economic growth.

Caught between these two positions are entrepreneurship and the question of how it affects QOL. Entrepreneurship is not only the major source of economic growth, it is also the major source of solutions to the dysfunctional outcomes growth produces. Stated differently, entrepreneurship is both the problem and the solution. Entrepreneurship enhances QOL (principally through the economic dimension) but in the process contributes to problems that detract from QOL (e.g., through the social and ecological dimensions). Yet it represents the best hope for addressing the problems that it helped create (e.g., through the technological dimension). By letting this state of affairs persist in the United States, societal QOL has continually improved. Figure 8.1 captures the relationships suggested here. Also included is a feedback loop, as there is some evidence that suggests entrepreneurship is fostered where QOL is better (Pennings,1982).

Conversely, if entrepreneurship is eliminated, or severely constrained, will growth be substantially reduced? If so, will environmental problems, such as pollution and resource depletion, either resolve themselves or become less serious? The answer to the first question is clearly yes. Considerable evidence exists that economic growth rates are slower in societies with a limited or nonexistent entrepreneurial sector, and higher in those with more entrepreneurship (Gilder, 1984; Hofstede, 1980; Hoselitz, 1960; Hughes, 1986; Wilken, 1979).

With regard to the second question, the answer would appear to be no. Populations will continue to grow, scarce resources will be consumed, pollution will be produced, and the haves will continue to want more and be unwilling to give to the have-nots. Revelations regarding the status of various QOL dimen-

Figure 8.1
A Dynamic Model of Entrepreneurship and QOL

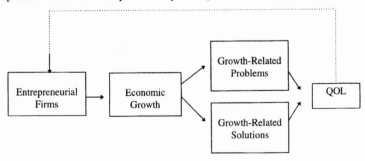

sions following the demise of communist regimes in the countries that once
formed the Soviet Union and its Eastern European satellites (where entrepreneurial sectors were severely limited) would seem to support this conclusion.

Under these circumstances, where will the solutions come from? The non-
entrepreneurial segments of the business community will not produce solutions,
nor will the non-profit institutions of society, which would find themselves in
an increasingly underfunded state. The remaining source of solutions would be
the government, whose policies have often tended to magnify rather than resolve
such problems (Maurice and Smithson, 1984; see also Chapter Nine). Moreover,
governments are highly inefficient at developing and manufacturing products
and services that eliminate pollution, slow birth rates, or replace natural resources. As we saw, especially in the cases of Chile and Singapore, enlightened
government's principal contribution is to facilitate coherent growth strategies
built around a dynamic entrepreneurial sector.

CONCLUSIONS

The ability of a nation to achieve and sustain economic prosperity is dependent upon how well it supports the development and allocation of the innate
entrepreneurial potential of its people and organizations. We believe in a bottom-
up perspective, wherein the vast majority of entrepreneurial behavior derives
from individual action and free choice by society's members.

However, there must also be a vision from the top. A country's leaders must
espouse a clear philosophy regarding entrepreneurship. They must delineate
where the country seeks to be in terms of the entrepreneurial grid (see Chapter
4) and formulate a national strategy for accomplishing this position. Such a
strategy provides a long-term guide to determining the desired rates of growth,
levels of risk exposure, and degrees of innovativeness in the economy.

This is not an argument for government to plan or control the economy.
Actually, just the opposite is needed. Enlightened government consists of leaders
who know how to provide a vision, and who can design rules and rewards that
reinforce that vision, while getting out of the way by letting individuals and
organizations act on their own entrepreneurial potential in their own way. The
purpose of government becomes one of steering, not rowing, and of building
an enabling infrastructure.

Determining the appropriate level of EI at the societal level also requires an
understanding of the linkages between entrepreneurship and societal well-being
or QOL. As we have argued, each of the dimensions, or domains, of the QOL
experienced by members of a society is affected both positively and negatively
by entrepreneurship. The relative importance of these dimensions is likely to
vary depending on the values and the stage of economic development of a
nation. Correspondingly, the saliency placed on a given functional or dysfunctional outcome of entrepreneurship can be expected to differ across countries.

In the final analysis, it is not a question of whether to emphasize entrepreneurial intensity, but how strongly. This conclusion is based on a dynamic model of societal entrepreneurship, in which EI is recognized as the source of growth and dynamism, as the creator of growth-related problems, and as a source of the solutions to these problems.

REFERENCES

Birch, D.L. 1981. "Who Creates Jobs?" *The Public Interest*, 65 (Fall), 62–82.

Baumol, W.J. 1990. "Entrepreneurship: Productive, Unproductive, and Destructive." *Journal of Political Economy*, 98 (5), Part 1: 893–921.

Beerman, K. 1996. "Moving On—Chile's Alternatives to NAFTA." *Harvard International Review*, 18 (3), 64–69.

Bosworth, B.P. et al. 1994. *The Chilean Economy: Policy Lessons and Challenges.* Washington, DC: Brookings Institution.

Campbell, A. et al. 1976. *The Quality of American Life: Perceptions, Evaluations and Satisfactions.* New York: Russell Sage Foundation.

Davidsson, P. 1992. *Environment and Entrepreneurship: Culture, Structure, and New Firm Formation Rates in Sweden.* Paper presented at ENDEC World Conference on Entrepreneurship, Singapore (August).

Day, R.L. 1987. "Relationships Between Life Satisfaction and Consumer Satisfaction." In A.C. Samli (ed.), *Marketing and the Quality-of-Life Interface.* Westport, CT: Quorum Books, 289–311.

Drucker, P. 1985. *Innovation and Entrepreneurship: Practices and Principles.* New York: Harper and Row.

Enis, B.M. 1987. "Growth Without Limits: A Marketing Perspective on Twenty-First Century Quality of Life." In A.C. Samli (ed.), *Marketing and the Quality-of-Life Interface.* Westport, CT: Quorum Books, 139–152.

Ferguson, C.H. 1988. "From the People Who Brought You Voodoo Economics." *Harvard Business Review*, 66 (May–June), 55–62.

Foster, R. 1986. *Innovation: The Attacker's Advantage.* New York: Summit.

Gilder, G. 1984. *The Spirit of Enterprise.* New York: Simon and Schuster.

Granzin, K.L. 1987. " A General Systems Framework for Quality of Life." In A.C. Samli (ed.), *Marketing and the Quality-of-Life Interface.* Westport, CT: Quorum Books, 15–46.

Hofstede, G. 1980. "Motivation, Leadership, and Organizations: Do American Theories Apply Abroad?" *Organizational Dynamics*, 9 (Summer), 42–63.

Hoselitz, B.F. 1960. "The Early History of Entrepreneurial Theory." In J.J. Spengler and W.R. Allen (eds.), *Essays in Economic Thought: Aristotle to Marshall.* Chicago: Rand McNally, 234–258.

Hughes, J. 1986. *The Vital Few: The Entrepreneur and American Economic Progress.* New York: Oxford University Press.

Kaplan, R. 1987. "Entrepreneurship Reconsidered: The Antimanagement Bias." *Harvard Business Review*, 65 (May–June), 84–89.

Kets de Vries, Manfred, F.R. 1984. "The Dark Side of Entrepreneurship." *Harvard Business Review*, 63 (November–December), 160–7.

Mallaby, S. 1995. "South Korea: Quick, Quick, Quick." *Economist*, 335 (7917) (June), SS3–SS5.

Maslow, A.H. 1970. *Motivation and Personality*, 2nd ed. New York: Harper and Row.

Maurice, C., and Smithson, C.W. 1984. *The Doomsday Myth*. Palo Alto, CA: Hoover Institution Press.

Meadows, D.H. et al. 1972. *The Limits to Growth*. New York: Universe Books.

"The Miracle Unmasked." 1995. *The Economist* (December), 4–6.

Pennings, J.M. 1982. "The Urban Quality of Life and Entrepreneurship." *Academy of Management Journal*, 25, 63–79.

Pilling, D. 1994. "Chile's Champion of Stability." *Euromoney*, 305 (September), 286–287.

Reich, R.B. 1987. "Entrepreneurship Reconsidered: The Team as Hero." *Harvard Business Review*, 65 (May–June), 77–83.

Rice, R.W. et al. 1985. "Organizational Work and The Perceived Quality of Life: Toward A Conceptual Model." *Academy of Management Review*, 10, 296–310.

Schumacher, E.F. 1973. *Small Is Beautiful: Economics As If People Mattered*. New York: Harper and Row.

Schumpeter, J. 1950. *Capitalism, Socialism, and Democracy*. New York: Harper and Row.

Sirgy, M.J. et al. 1985. "The Question of Value in Social Marketing: Use of a Quality of Life Theory to Achieve Long-Term Life Satisfaction." *The American Journal of Economics and Sociology*, 44 (April), 215–228.

Tang, H.K. and Yeo, K.T. 1995. "Technology, Entrepreneurship and National Development: Lessons from Singapore." *International Journal of Technology Management*, 10 (7–8), 797–814.

Tucker, R.C. 1978. *The Marx-Engels Reader*, 2nd ed. New York: Norton Publishing.

Veblen, T. 1967. *The Theory of the Leisure Class*. New York: Viking Press.

Wilken, P.H. 1979. *Entrepreneurship: A Comparative and Historical Study*. Norwood, NJ: Ablex.

Withey, S.B. 1972. "Values and Social Change." In B. Strumpel (ed.), *Subjective Elements of Well-Being*. Paris: Organization for Economic Cooperation and Development.

Young, J. 1985. "Global Competition: The New Reality." *California Management Review*, 28 (Spring), 11–25.

9

Government and Entrepreneurship

INTRODUCTION

The major theme of this book concerns the need for public policy makers, education officials, business executives, and community leaders to create environments that facilitate entrepreneurial intensity at the individual, organizational, and societal levels. Government policy is especially critical here, for as Baumol (1990, p. 894) notes, "How the entrepreneur acts at a given time and place depends heavily on the rules of the game—the reward structure in the economy—that happen to prevail." Unfortunately, the orientation of current public policy is to create a pernicious set of rules that effectively discourages entrepreneurship while tacitly supporting small business start-ups.

IN FAVORING SMALL BUSINESS, GOVERNMENT IGNORES ENTREPRENEURSHIP

Small business owners and lobbyists have maintained for many years that most social regulations, antitrust laws, securities regulations, and intellectual property laws have a detrimental effect on small businesses. Many of the regulations in environmental protection, labor standards, and tax policy have extremely negative implications for the competitive abilities of small firms.

Weidenbaum (1992) calculated that regulation adds over $400 billion to private-sector costs, and Susbauer (1981) has estimated that regulatory paperwork alone adds as much as $20 billion to small business costs. Singh et al. (1987) demonstrated that small businesses pay the highest effective corporate tax rates. Others point out that small businesses also suffer because they can ill afford litigation when accused of a potential regulatory violation.

There is no question that regulatory policies create significant hardships for small businesses. However, it is the growth-oriented business that is most heavily penalized. The reality is that regulatory constraints serve only to inflate the costs associated with growth. These costs fall into two major categories: compliance costs and innovation costs.

The costs of regulatory compliance include legal fees for interpretation of regulations, consultant fees for recommendations on meeting regulatory requirements, costs associated with actually complying with applicable regulations (e.g., labor, material, equipment), costs of generating and maintaining documentation of compliance, and costs of staff for reporting and filing compliance documents. While compliance costs are potentially high for any firm, such regulations are often regressive in nature and thus of greater consequence to the bottom line of small businesses. Thus, Sommers and Cole (1981) have provided empirical evidence that the cost of compliance per unit sold or service provided is higher in small businesses than in mid-size or large organizations. The Batelle Human Affairs Research Center estimates that it costs businesses with fewer than 50 employees seven to ten times as much to comply as it does larger firms. As a result, compliance costs may reduce the small firm's ability to compete effectively, and the long-term effect of this can range from lost business to the demise of the firm (Berney and Swanson, 1982; McKee, 1992).

While these arguments are quite compelling, extensive lobbying efforts by small business advocates have helped protect most small businesses from mandatory compliance with many regulatory requirements. Although the definition of small varies among regulatory agencies, a perusal of the Environmental Protection Agency (EPA), Occupational Safety and Health Administration (OSHA), Equal Employment Opportunity Commission (EEOC), Labor Department, and Internal Revenue Service (IRS) rules suggests that many small firms are exempt or otherwise receive favorable treatment. Many special exemptions exist for particular industries or firms faced with certain prescribed circumstances.

Few would dispute that compliance exclusions for small businesses are essential for their competitive viability and for incubating certain infant industries. But these exclusions may have an unintended consequence: they can be a disincentive for growth. Entrepreneurial firms with a growth orientation find that to grow means to be subjected to costly regulations that significantly reduce their profitability while exacerbating what is typically already a critical cash-flow shortage.

A growth-oriented small business must at some point surpass the upper limits of the regulatory exclusions as it increases its sales, the number of its employees, the payroll deductions it processes, or the waste that it generates. The firm thus becomes exposed to regulatory policy from which it was protected before it grew. Compliance often requires excessive expenditures that seem unjustifiable in the face of other costs associated with growth. The entrepreneurial firm must balance the perceived benefits of growth against the perceived risks and also factor in the very tangible costs imposed via public policy. While small firms are able to pursue a strategy of partial compliance (Sommers and Cole, 1981), entrepreneurial firms are not. Because their violations are more difficult to detect, small firms may simply choose not to comply. This option is less realistic for growth-oriented firms, for growth itself serves to heighten their visibility.

Less tangible but equally important, are innovation costs. These are the opportunity costs of foregoing new technologies, products, and services that would require compliance with regulations. Burdened by excessive and sometimes incomprehensible policies regulating the entry into new industry or product categories, many growth-oriented businesses simply choose not to innovate.

Even large growth-oriented firms may be stifled by excessive government regulation. Consider, for example, how the FDA's complicated process for approving new biotechnology has hindered advances in agriculture. Further, regulatory restrictions on the telecommunications industry were faulted for the U.S.'s lag in developing fiber optics and high-definition television (Warner, 1992). In the final analysis, while the tangible monetary costs of regulatory compliance are quite high, the costs of lost opportunities for economic growth and innovation are probably the most significant, especially in terms of the long-term impact on societal quality of life (see Chapter 8).

THE DANGEROUS DIRECTION OF PUBLIC POLICY

Of perhaps even greater concern is the overall trend in regulation. Quite simply, the creation of government rules and tax constraints represents a growth industry. Consider a few examples.

In recent years, government policy has effectively placed employers in the health-care business. This has come at a time when health-care costs have increased at a relentless pace far exceeding the annual rate of inflation. As the burden of health insurance continues to grow, enterprises are forced to compromise on their growth ambitions because new employees become artificially overpriced.

Product liability has also shifted dramatically away from consumers and toward manufacturers. Legal remedies for injured consumers have broadened, and the scope of manufacturer culpability has expanded. As a result, companies today are held liable for damages regardless of how much the consumer misuses or abuses the product, fails to follow clearly visible instructions, or otherwise does not exercise common sense. Not surprisingly, the number of suits filed in federal and state courts is increasing at a double-digit annual pace. As a result, Begley (1995) notes that 47% of surveyed companies withdrew products from markets because of fears of litigation, and 25% discontinued a line of research. Obviously, the companies that innovate more are the most vulnerable to such a total liability philosophy. This creates an incentive for firms to concentrate instead on imitative, "me-too," innovation, where established products are changed incrementally.

Another example concerns affirmative action requirements. A significant move away from the original intentions of affirmative action has occurred as government has sought not only to monitor but to direct the private discretionary and voluntary actions of individuals and organizations. Thus, the focus today is on effective quotas (with companies subject to litigation on the grounds of de facto underrepresentation of a given minority class proportional to the population). Diluted, race-normed examinations, gender-normed selection criteria, and racial and gender set-asides that guarantee an increasingly disproportionate percentage of government contracts for protected classes have been introduced. The result is a spoils system that promotes group rights over individual merit. Such programs foster bitter resentment and heightened polarization of the citizenry, leading to accusations that relatively under-qualified employees are being hired, which undermines the principles of merit, efficiency, and cost-effectiveness. Further, beneficiaries of these programs are often stereotyped as not having earned their positions; as a result, they may be ostracized and placed on a slow promotion track.

Growing constraints on entrepreneurial behavior can also be seen in the environmental area. In 1994, Americans were spending over $125 billion or 2.5% of the gross national product (GNP) to comply with environmental statutes and regulations (Bowermaster and Gest, 1995). The EPA, with a staff of 18,000 and a yearly budget of $6.7 billion, consumes one-third of the federal regulatory budget. Such key environmental programs as the Clean Air Act, the Clean Water Act, and the Resource Conservation and Recovery Act are all top-down, command-and-control regulations (i.e., inflexible approaches that ignore market-based incentives or marketplace solutions). They tend to involve slow-moving and ill-informed processes, highly adversarial confrontations, inefficiencies (in that uniform standards fail to account for unique difficulties that arise in satisfying the requirements of different industries and regions of the country), and politicized decisions regarding whom to penalize when violations occur. The result is explosive litigation costs, deceptive increases in the price of goods, and overt bars against competition.

Antitrust regulation represents one final example of how regulation has come to serve as a mechanism to create barriers to market entry or to confer other special privileges. Antitrust essentially represents an effort not to expand but to suppress an objectively competitive market while restraining output and growth in productivity. In today's globally competitive marketplace, it is a severe impediment to innovation. These regulations assume a naive micro-economic analysis that ensures a "perfectly" competitive static paradigm, when it is *dynamic* competition that is relevant (Jorden and Teece, 1990). Dynamic competition issues from the development of new products, services, or processes. Antitrust negatively affects the ability of innovating firms to cooperate in their development and communication efforts and limits business strategies or inter-firm agreements to keep "me too" competitors at bay. In fact, antitrust has become much more favorable towards mergers than towards inter-firm agreements.

As government constraints on entrepreneurial growth continue to escalate, significant concerns should be raised about the long-term competitive viability of the U.S. economy, and by extension, the societal quality of life (QOL).

BUREAUCRACY AND THE ANTI-ENTREPRENEURIAL BIAS OF GOVERNMENT

Government at all levels is inherently anti-entrepreneurial. Fundamental conflicts exist between the way government does business and the requirements of the start-up or the corporate entrepreneur. In fact, these conflicts undermine the very essence of entrepreneurship. Table 9.1 summarizes twelve of these conflicts.

While this bias can be traced to a number of factors (e.g., value systems of those attracted to public service), the endemic nature of this bias is related to government's continued reliance on a bureaucratic model of organization.

Numerous theoretical perspectives on bureaucracy have been offered over the years (see Etzioni-Halevey, 1983; Wiggs, 1994; and Wittergreen 1988, for a more detailed treatment of these perspectives). Regardless of the perspective, bureaucracy as a form of government organization is threatened by an entrepreneurial person or firm that acts as an agent of change. While the entrepreneur as a start-up or mom-and-pop business proprietor can typically be ignored, the entrepreneur as a growth-oriented innovator cannot be.

Modern bureaucracy has developed at least fourteen key characteristics that make it incompatible with high levels of entrepreneurial intensity (EI) (Averch, 1990; Howard, 1968; Stein, 1995). These can be summarized as follows:

Pluralism. Administrative agencies are boxed in by intricately related and often strongly opposing interests. To survive, they must take into account, and be responsive to, all politically effective groups, any number of which may have problems with the change wrought by an entrepreneurial enterprise. The bureaucracy becomes a contending and offsetting collection of fiefdoms.

Overload. The revolution in entitlements over the past 50 years has produced an expectation by dependent groups that the government is the first resort for their well-being. Increasing demands have made the government increasingly unable to cope. The more decisions it must handle, the more it becomes hostage to political and governmental influences.

Rational Limited Search. Bureaucracies fail to seek the most effective solutions and concentrate on precedent and standard operating procedures. Unlike entrepreneurs, they do not seek the greatest level of performance for the least cost. Similarly, faced with uncertainty, they do not estimate the relevant probability distribution of various outcomes and apply the appropriate discount rates to maximize rates of return to society.

Multiple Objectives and Constituencies. Bureaucrats rarely ask, "Who is our market?" Enabling legislation for the programs they administer often contains vague and conflicting objectives because of the necessity to achieve consensus. Moreover, growth-oriented enterprises are rarely included on any list of possible constituencies to be served.

Table 9.1
Summary of Twelve Conflicts between the Orientation of Government and Requirements of Entrepreneurship

	Government Orientation	Entrepreneurial Requirement
1	Standardized approaches and operating procedures	Need for flexible approaches to reflect novel circumstances
2	Compromise among the conflicting objectives of multiple constituencies	Sole focus on growth and innovation as the means to other societal ends
3	Focus on process, how things are done	Concerned with outcomes, what gets done
4	Approaches tied to short-term budget cycles (1-2 years)	Concern is life of a project or opportunity
5	Largely unconcerned about costs of compliance with its decisions	Costs of compliance detract from competitiveness and ability to create value for customers
6	Absolutist approach to remedying a societal ill	Need for trade-offs in flexibly developing innovative solutions
7	Risk-aversive	Calculated risk-taking
8	Side-effects of innovation must be minimized	Net benefits of innovation should outweigh costs of the innovation and its side-effects
9	Slow, ponderous decision process involving extensive consultation and transparency	Quick decisions to reflect short windows of opportunity
10	Growth as disruptive and a source of problems	Growth as the objective
11	Resource-driven	Opportunity-driven
12	Adversarial approach to dealing with private sector	Willingness to partner with government in addressing opportunities

Uncertain Production Functions. It is very difficult to measure the efficiency or effectiveness of bureaucratic performance. The production function is only partially known. A bureaucracy rarely knows what would happen if it employed alternative combinations of inputs. There is little incentive to experiment to see if the organizational design, the staff, and the technology used can be varied to increase, let alone maximize, output.

Input-Output Measures. Because performance tends to be measured by the amount of inputs from sponsors or publics, not by indicators of output or government impact, bureaucracies design programs, and conspire with clients and constituents, to achieve more staff and budget. Should the bureaucracy request fewer inputs, its client groups are apt to accuse it of dishonoring its mandate, while lower budget requests (e.g., due to productivity gains or problem resolution) invite even greater cuts the next time around.

Need for Symbols. Besides their stated objectives, bureaucracies have symbolic and "signaling" objectives. Since a bureaucracy's sponsor faces conflicting claims and limited resources, bureaucracies will seek the most visible programs to justify their budget requests. Even though effectiveness may depend on concentrating resource expenditures, political pressures may dilute how expenditures are actually allocated.

Equity vs. Effectiveness. Bureaucracies must make program trade-offs between effectiveness and equity. They tend to start a new program or initiative with an ostensibly effective design and rational criteria, but soon pressure is exerted to expand eligibility or entitlement. Unlike in the marketplace, those excluded from benefits find that bureaucracy itself becomes the vehicle for redress. So perverse is the syndrome that equity per se becomes the objective of most government programs. By emphasizing equity, flexible solutions that differentiate and reinforce the contributions of growth-oriented enterprises are not possible.

Budget Cycles and Floors. Bureaucracies operate with one- or two-year budget cycles that compress the need to justify the level of resources they receive and amplify the need to expand those resources. There is a built-in incentive to allocate resources to marginal projects. Unspent or unobligated funds cannot be rationalized. Attempts to cut budgets will only make the bureaucracies seek new constituencies that must be served. Staff reduction will result in potentially more money being spent on temporary personnel or outsourcing.

Tenure of Senior Decision-Makers. High-level managers, especially political appointees, have short tenure and no ownership claims on the organization. Perceived short-term success (e.g., expanding the budget) is often more important than long-term success (solving the problem).

Sunk Costs. In the private sector, sunk costs are not allocated to current operations but are recovered over a product's life cycle. In a bureaucracy, when sunk costs do not generate positive outcomes over time, the problem is explained not as too much money expended, but as too little.

Random Agenda Solution. Bureaucrats are driven by a combination of publicity concerns, pressure from and reporting requirements of funding bodies, agitation by public-interest organizations, and random developments. The agenda emphasized at a given time will vary depending upon the overriding source of influence.

Tunnel Vision. Bureaucracies bring an extreme perspective to risk-taking. Unable to see how any particular risk fits into the overall range of risks in the world, they fail to consider trade-off possibilities. Instead, they are obsessed with the last 10%. They insist not on reasonableness but on complete solutions to a given societal problem.

Inconsistency. Regulations do not deal with risks of similar magnitude in similar ways. At one extreme, the EPA's ban on asbestos might cost $250 million to save eight lives over thirteen years. At the other extreme, disease screening and vaccination programs may save lives at a cost of $50,000 to $70,000 each. Bureaucratic rules allow little leeway to adjust procedures to specific cases.

These fourteen characteristics make it impossible for bureaucracies to do anything but hinder entrepreneurship efforts; therefore, greater EI is met with more bureaucratic resistance. Entrepreneurship threatens bureaucracy to the extent that it represents a significant reallocation of resources, makes existing rules (and government jobs) irrelevant and obsolete, and demands novel public-sector solutions. From a QOL perspective (see Chapter 8), government bureaucracies focus only on the dysfunctional aspects of growth that result from entrepreneurial efforts, even at the expense of functional aspects.

TOWARD ENTREPRENEURIAL GOVERNMENT

In these chapters, we have argued that entrepreneurship is an environmentally driven phenomenon and that it is the major force for improvements in societal QOL. While there are other influences, government has a lead role in affecting the environment for entrepreneurship. Unfortunately, its actual role tends to be problematic. Mired in process, driven by often conflicting goals, resistant to change, and defining success by inputs rather than results, government bodies inevitably adopt "one size fits all" policies, and this places tremendous costs on entrepreneurial individuals and organizations.

What is needed is a fairly radical redefinition of the role of government in the economy. The neoclassical or laissez-faire conceptualization of government's role emphasized limiting interference to activities that fostered competitiveness or made the free market operate more efficiently, and to those necessary functions that the private marketplace could not be expected to adequately carry out. The significant expansion of government involvement during the twentieth century has come in response to a number of concerns, many of which have little to do with enhancing economic freedom or improving the economic dimension of QOL. In fact, the explicit focus appears to be on the non-economic QOL dimensions. Examples of such concerns include controlling the spillover costs that result from normal business operations, redistribution of income from haves to have-nots, redressing employment-related civil rights violations, and improving workers' safety, health, and family lifestyles.

While the regulated areas are fairly similar in most advanced industrial societies, the U.S. is unique in the way regulation is accomplished. Compared to other developed nations, U.S. regulatory authorities impose more detailed rules and interpretations, more paperwork, more formal inspections and reports, and significantly higher compliance costs. Thus, Puryear and Wiggins (1981) observed that some 90 federal agencies issue about 7,000 new rules each year. Weidenbaum (1992) noted funding for 122,400 regulators in the 1992 federal budget. Consistent with our earlier argument, Kristol (1978) suggests that regulatory agencies are staffed with career employees who share an antipathy toward business and the free market system. They bring zeal and aggressiveness to the regulatory task, while trying to redistribute power from the private to the public sector.

It is our position that government efforts to facilitate the non-economic dimensions of QOL actually come at the expense of both the economic as well as the non-economic QOL dimensions to the extent that these efforts hinder entrepreneurial behavior. The fact that many governmental actions have mixed and seemingly contradictory effects may reflect the absence of a consistent philosophy or ideological foundation on which to base these actions. Ironically, as its involvement level has expanded, the role and objectives of government in the private sector have become more obscure.

Several modern schools of thought exist regarding the role of government. One of the more prominent contemporary perspectives that is noticeably anti-entrepreneurial has been put forward by a number of scholars from the Massachusetts Institute of Technology (MIT) and Harvard University (Ferguson, 1988; Lawrence and Dyer, 1983; Reich, 1987). They argue for more collaboration between government and big business, ostensibly to generate national industrial plans and policies. Centralization and standardization are cornerstones of this philosophy. Entrepreneurial firms are viewed as counterproductive entities responsible for selling off America's public assets and undermining the competitiveness of mainstream industries.

We believe the opposite course must be pursued. The central objective of public policies directed at the private sector should be to facilitate entrepreneurial behavior. It is not a big business or small business issue, but instead, one of singling out entrepreneurs and entrepreneurial firms as focal points for regulatory support. As such, the central tenets of government policy should be decentralization, flexibility, and specialization or customization.

Decentralization refers to the need to move administrative decision making closer to the entrepreneur. In many decision areas, federal responsibility should be reassigned to states and locales. Within the organizational structures at each level, greater discretionary freedom should be extended to mid-level and even low-level bureaucrats so they can waive regulations if they deem them inappropriate for a given situation. Such *flexibility* must also be applied to the entire question of risk. Total risk to society must be considered when constraining entrepreneurial efforts, and reasonable trade-offs must be made (1) among categories or types of risks, and (2) between societal benefits and costs. *Specialization* implies a need for government to segment its markets and tailor unique programs and solutions to differing markets. It also suggests that government bodies should take on fewer and more fundamental tasks and return as many questions relative to risk-taking to the marketplace, where, as von Mises (1944) argued, decision-makers are not free from the economic consequences of their policies and must act accordingly.

This approach means developing programs of incentives and limited restraints for business segments that accomplish growth, regardless of the industry they are in. It also means customized programs that give incentives to entrepreneurs to concentrate on products and services that address the dysfunctional aspects of conventional entrepreneurship (e.g., pollution, resource depletion). In both cases, policies favoring proactive competition, innovation, risk-sharing, organizational autonomy, and the search for long-term profits are critical. Regulatory agencies must also be free to select from among competing regulatory solutions while favoring entrepreneurial incentives over penalties. Moreover, they must be held accountable for demonstrating that benefits of a given regulatory solution exceed costs.

More fundamentally, the bureaucratic model itself must be abandoned in favor of an entrepreneurial model of governance. The prescriptions of the recent literature on reinventing government represent a good first step in this direction (see Chapter 7). The essence of these proposals is that a number of free-market principles can and should be applied to public-sector management, including competition, the price mechanism, management of the forces of supply and demand, a customer orientation, and the leveraging of resources. But our position is that things should be taken even further.

The culture of public organizations must be changed to emphasize the values of innovation, calculated risk-taking, and proactive behavior. The goal should be to creatively respond to targeted customer segments, and entrepreneurial enterprises should be the priority. Entrepreneurial enterprises should also be considered as partners, not adversaries. By removing all obstacles to entrepreneurial growth, while concentrating resource deployment on further developing the educational, financial, social, legal, and logistical structures so as to enable entrepreneurial intensity, government will contribute significantly to the enhancement of societal QOL. Since QOL is a moving target, public policy must be able to rapidly adapt to emerging societal opportunities. Perhaps the key to accomplishing such an orientation lies in getting public-policy administrators to view themselves as entrepreneurs, and the process of regulation as an entrepreneurial undertaking.

CONCLUSIONS

Government policy-makers would appear to distinguish small organizations from large ones, and profit-seeking from not-for-profit ones. They make a distinction among organizations based on whether they are capital- or labor-intensive, and what industry grouping they fall into. However, when it comes to growth and innovation, there is a noticeable silence. Government targets little in the way of incentives, rewards, or regulatory support to organizations that achieve or sustain high rates of growth or contribute significant innovations. Actually, just the opposite is the case.

Overcoming the anti-entrepreneurial bias of government requires a revolution in the public sector no different from the one that is underway in the private sector. Corporations are unbundling, restructuring, reengineering, downsizing, empowering, and outsourcing. But more than this, fundamental questions are being raised about their relationships with suppliers, competitors, and customers. Traditional theory is under assault.

The same challenges confront government. Traditional structures and roles are being challenged. Bureaucracy as a model for governing is obsolete. We are not suggesting a need for less bureaucracy but instead, for a new model based on partnerships, decentralization, flexibility, and specialization or customization. Government as regulator and watchdog must be replaced by government as facilitator of entrepreneurial solutions to such problems as product safety, crime, environmental protection (enhancement), and labor market discrimination. The tax and regulator penalties should be targeted at those who fail to innovate, while protective support must be taken away from those who fail to create growth or find new sources of value.

REFERENCES

Averch, H. 1990. *Private Markets and Public Intervention: A Primer for Policy Designers*. Pittsburgh, PA: University of Pittsburgh Press.

Baumol, W.J. 1990. "Entrepreneurship: Productive, Unproductive, and Destructive." *Journal of Political Economy*, 98 (5), Part 1, 893–921.

Begley, R. 1995. "Product Liability: Reform at Last." *Chemical Week*, 2 (August), 5.

Berney, R. and Swanson, J. 1982. "The Regressive Impact of Governmental Regulations: Some Theoretical and Empirical Evidence." *American Journal of Small Business*, 51 (3), 16–25.

Bowermaster, D., and Gest, T. 1995. "Say You Want a Revolution." *U.S. News and World Report*, 119 (14), 38–41.

Etzioni-Halevy, E. 1983. *Bureaucracy and Democracy: A Political Dilemma*. London: Routledge and Kegan Paul.

Ferguson, C.H. 1988. "From the People Who Brought You Voodoo Economics." *Harvard Business Review*, 66 (May–June), 55–62.

Howard, P.K. 1968. *The Death of Common Sense: How Law Is Suffocating America*. New York: Random House.

Jorden, T.M., and Teece, D.J. 1990. "Innovation, Dynamic Competition, and Antitrust Policy." *CATO Review of Business and Government* (Fall), 35–44.

Kristol, I. 1978. *Two Cheers for Capitalism*. New York: Basic Books.

Lawrence, P., and Dyer, D. 1983. *Renewing American Industry: Organizing for Efficiency and Innovation*. New York: The Free Press.

Litan, R., and Nordhaus, W. 1983. *Reforming Federal Regulation*. New Haven, CT: Yale University Press.

McKee, B. 1992. "Environmental Price Tags." *Nation's Business* (April), 36–38.

Puryear, A.N., and Wiggins, C.P. 1981. "The Impact of Federal Regulations." In *The Environment for Entrepreneurship and Small Business: Summary Analysis of the Regional Research Reports*. Washington, DC: U.S. Small Business Administration, Office of Advocacy, 50–51.

Reich, R.B. 1987. "Entrepreneurship Reconsidered: The Team as Hero." *Harvard Business Review*, 65 (May–June), 77–83.

Singh, D., Wilder, R.P., and Chan, K.P. 1987. "Tax Rates in Small and Large Firms." *American Journal of Small Business* (Fall), 41–51.

Sommers, P., and Cole, R. 1981. "Costs of Compliance in Small and Medium-Sized Businesses." *American Journal of Small Business*, 51 (1), 25–29.

Stein, J. 1995. "Building a Better Bureaucrat." *Regulation*, 3, 24–33.

Susbauer, J.C. 1981. "The Impact of Federal Regulations." In *The Environment for*

Entrepreneurship and Small Business: Summary Analysis of the Regional Research Reports. Washington, DC: U.S. Small Business Administration, Office of Advocacy, 108–109.

Von Mises, L. 1944. *Bureaucracy.* New Haven, CT: Yale University Press.

Warner, D. 1992. "Regulations, Staggering Costs." *Nation's Business* (June), 50–54.

Weidenbaum, M. 1992. "Return of the 'R' Word." *Policy Review* (Winter), 40–53.

Wiggs, F.W. 1994. "Bureaucracy and the Constitution." *Public Administration Review*, (January–February), 65–72.

Wittergreen, J.A. 1988. "The Regulatory Revolution and the New Bureaucratic State." *The Heritage Lectures*, 10 (August), 1–13.

10

A Braver New World: Entrepreneurship and the Future

INTRODUCTION

What does the future hold? Obviously, no one knows for sure. Even those who specialize in spotting trends and extrapolating them have very different views on what will happen, much less when, where, and how it will happen. Yet, there are some areas of general agreement, and we will explore those, and their implications for entrepreneurial behavior, in this chapter.

As a beginning point, we believe one thing is certain: turbulence. The environments surrounding individuals, organizations, and societies are only likely to become more turbulent in the next two decades. Specifically, it would seem reasonable to expect that:

- technological change will *not* slow down and *will not* become less complex as existing and emerging technologies are integrated;
- markets will *not* become more homogeneous with fewer segments or niches;
- competition is *unlikely* to become more passive or predictable;
- governments will *not* impose fewer regulations on business;
- social values are *not* likely to be challenged less; social diversity is *not* apt to diminish;
- employees will *not* become more passive, and critical skills needed by companies will *not* be in greater abundance;
- resource prices and availability will *not* fluctuate less.

In fact, dramatic change is probably going to be the case in each of these areas. The implications for the entrepreneur are two-fold. First, turbulence creates disturbances or threats to the existing approach, the status quo, and the conventional wisdom. The fundamental need becomes greater for entrepreneurs who can find opportunity within these threats or develop innovative solutions that address these threats. More succinctly, in the future we shall all have to be entrepreneurs or at least tap much more of the entrepreneurial potential that resides within us. Secondly, threats will not only become more numerous, they will come more quickly and be of less predictable duration. This means entrepreneurs will have to be able to move quicker and adapt more readily to capitalize on emerging opportunities.

THE PROGNOSTICATORS

There are many trend spotters and predictors of the future, or futurists, who try to bring order to the turbulence. In fact, given the sales of such books as *Megatrends* (Naisbitt and Aburdene, 1990), *The Popcorn Report* (Popcorn, 1991), and *The Age of Unreason* (Handy, 1989), it would seem that futurism is an entrepreneurial growth industry (which is not surprising in turbulent times). Let us examine the work of four of the leading prognosticators.

One of the most popular of the futurists is Charles Handy. He has written a series of books that attempt to prepare us for a new way of life that is, in many ways, already upon us. One of his premises is that we live in an era of increasing paradox, where we are confronted with seemingly contradictory circumstances (Handy, 1994). Table 10.1 summarizes these paradoxes, each of which has important implications for entrepreneurship.

For example, entrepreneurs will increasingly find that their intellect and openness to continuous learning are not only competitive weapons but represent the fundamental source of value creation in any venture. Their most critical (ongoing) investment will be in people, who themselves will prove to be less permanent or loyal, and the skills and intellectual capital of these employees will become "obsolete" more quickly. The growth of the do-it-yourself and informal markets present a host of entrepreneurial opportunities. Examples include businesses targeting the "self" concept (e.g., self-publishing, self-training, do-it-yourself (d-i-y) home repair) and those that sell support services to this market (e.g., telephone answering services, office rentals by the day, temporary computer access services). Perceived time shortages suggest opportunities for those who can operate on a real-time basis, with shortened order cycle times and a willingness to be accessible 24 hours a day. Further, organizational paradoxes suggest that entrepreneurial companies will take hybrid forms, with extremely flat structures, organizational charts with curves and circles instead of lines or boxes, and extended external networks. As discussed in Chapter 6, a key objective will be to balance individual drive and vision against the need for cooperative teams of generalists and specialists.

To the paradoxes in Table 10.1, Naisbitt (1994, p. 1) adds one more. He argues that "the bigger the world economy, the more powerful its smallest players." In a mass production era, economies of scale, standardization, and

Table 10.1
Handy's Nine Paradoxes

Paradox 1:
Intelligence, which has none of the characteristics typically associated with property (cannot be redistributed, owned or taken away by someone else, valued on balance sheets, is owned by everyone) is property. The ability to acquire and apply knowledge becomes the source of value creation and wealth.

Paradox 2:
People either have work and money but no time, or no work or money but plenty of time. Those without jobs or time do not have the tools to create their own employment opportunities. A divided society results from the dilemma of choosing between fewer, better-paid, better-educated, better-protected workers, or more but cheaper ones.

Paradox 3:
Productivity concerns find more people forced into the do-it-yourself (d-i-y), informal or black market, where much of their economic contribution is not counted. The formal market no longer values their economic contributions, although the d-i-y, informal and black markets may represent the major source of economic growth in society.

Paradox 4:
Technology and productivity improvements mean we leave longer and it takes less time to accomplish most tasks, and yet people seem to have less free time.

Paradox 5:
Growing wealth in developed countries has produced a decline in births, which means fewer customers domestically. Growth can only come from exporting to less developed countries who cannot afford to buy from, and instead need to sell to, the developed countries. Thus, one must invest in one's potential competitors.

Paradox 6:
Companies must, at one and the same time, be global yet local, small yet large, centralized yet decentralized, planned yet flexible, differentiated yet integrated, standardized yet customized, with workers who are autonomous but team players.

Paradox 7:
Society's current generation sees itself as different from its predecessor, but plans for its children's generation to not differ from itself. Yet, the next generation will start work later, quit working earlier, will not be as scarred by war or nuclear threat, with children being planned and women's roles redefined.

Paradox 8:
Individualism requires teamwork, and teamwork requires individualism.

Paradox 9:
People must have an equal chance to achieve unequal rewards. Those who work hard and smart deserve to achieve more than others, but only if everyone has an equal opportunity to work hard and smart.

Source: Adapted from Handy (1994).

control typically defined success. But in the future, it will be networks of entrepreneurs that drive the system.

"Bigger is better" as a philosophy has already been replaced with an ethic that emphasizes flexibility, nimbleness, speed, and focus. Thus, the global economy will increasingly be dominated by small and medium-size enterprises, acting as part of cooperative networks. Many of these enterprises may be affiliates of multinational conglomerates, but traditionally large organizations will have "deconstructed" or downsized and reengineered themselves into confederations of smaller autonomous and highly aggressive units.

A very different perspective can be found in the work of Faith Popcorn and her Brain Reserve colleagues (1996). They identify sixteen trends that drive the consumer world. The trends are presented as a landscape, or framework, within which individuals can find where they and their ideas might fit or not fit. The authors demonstrate how an awareness of particular trends can serve as a launching point for a new venture. Table 10.2 illustrates a few of their trends and related business concepts that have been, or might be, successful.

Consider, as a case in point, Popcorn's concept of "anchoring." If people are looking for sources of stability and consistency, they might turn to religion. Pat Robertson (1996) foresees the decline of secular humanism and a growing role for God in our lives. This creates opportunities not only for churches (especially those who, understanding the 99 lives (see Table 10.2) trend, will schedule services and activities at flexible times) but for commercial entrepreneurs. Whether it is the mainstreaming of gospel music artists, sales of t-shirts with the pope's image on them, the marketing of weekend religious retreats at nature preserves, or the growth of the Family Channel (formerly the Christian Broadcast Network) on cable television, we find entrepreneurs at work capitalizing on the trend.

A third perspective is offered by Alvin Toffler (1990) and John Naisbitt (1990), who separately examine large societal shifts resulting from the transition to an information technology base from a manufacturing and industrial base. As illustrated in Table 10.3, these observers talk of dramatic developments in literally every walk of life. They argue that these are not idiosyncratic or random developments, but reflect an entirely new set of rules and assumptions (many of which are still being written or require continuous updating) in the post-industrial age.

As an example of the entrepreneurial potential that results from this transition, one has only to consider education. The move to an information-based society in which knowledge is power suggests a large growth in expenditures for employee training. Combining this with other trends, one can anticipate the privatization of training providers, the customization of training programs, training that focuses on the holistic individual, innovations so that training can be done at non-traditional times (e.g., in the middle of the night, or while driving), a speeding up of the delivery of training, new vehicles for training (e.g., interactive video), and training materials that more rapidly incorporate the newest insights

Table 10.2

A Sample of Popcorn's Trends and Their Application to Entrepreneurship

The Trend	Sample Entrepreneurial Concepts
"Cocooning" - stay at home more, build comfortable, secure environment in which can escape or be buffered and protected from a crazy world	• smart appliances • innovative lawn and garden tools • service providers (e.g., travel agents, medical testing companies) who come to your home • personal protection stun devices • home collect and deliver services • home security systems
"Anchoring" - desire for linkages to things stable, consistent, and secure from one's past; a guest for spiritual roots, religious ties, and self-identity	• genealogy-related products • meditation retreats • yoga centers • books, films, music focusing on miracles and angels • nature and gospel music • family networks and programming
"99 lives" - pace of life is so accelerated that each of us must increasingly fill multiple roles, work at multiple jobs, and undergo multiple changes at the same time	• beepers, pagers, cell phones, voice recorders, voicemail • instant news from anywhere available anytime • software to manage time, organize activities, manage personal finances • on-line banking, shopping, and schooling • e-mail
"Icon Toppling" - tendency to challenge or question our leaders, role models, pillars of society, authority figures, parents, police, and others	• alternative religious groups • private security services • anti-establishment designs in clothing, architecture, packaging • expose-all, tabloid TV, radio, newspapers, and books • anti-heroes featured in movies and as basis for new products and product endorsements
"Vigilante Consumer" - lack of trust in corporations, government and other institutions; general skepticism of advertising and sales claims; consumerism and a demand for better service, better products, better treatment, and more value for the money	• magazines telling people which products or vendors to boycott • devices to detect traces of (ostensibly illegal) drugs • systems to measure customer service levels • products/designs to reduce queuing or waiting times • new product labeling systems • interactive, on-line complaint handling systems
"Save Our Society" - a concern with environmentalism, including the depletion of natural resources, the extinction and abuse of animals and other species, air/water/noise/smoke pollution, overpopulation	• recycled products • natural products • biodegradable materials • noiseless dishwashers, vacuum cleaners, hand tools • paperless restaurants • ecotourism

Source: Adapted from Popcorn and Marigold (1996).

Table 10.3
Some of Naisbitt's "Megatrends" and Toffler's "Power Shifts"

- Booming global economy, free trade and trading blocks, growing economic interdependence
- Privatization and decline of the welfare state, devolution of state power
- Rise of the Pacific Rim and eastern values
- Advancement of democracy and democratic values
- Women in leadership, women as role models, emphasis on values of caring and sharing
- Age of biology/biotechnology
- Global lifestyles and cultural nationalism
- Renaissance of the arts, leisure, and escapism
- Multiple jobs, multiple careers, and part-time work
- Knowledge as power, serving as essence of financial or military power
- Decentralization, deconstruction, downsizing
- Fusion of producer and consumer
- Small runs of customized goods aimed at niche markets
- Higher levels of speed in everything; real-time simultaneity rather than sequential stages
- Electronic money, electronic transactions, electronic information
- Higher level of diversity combined with more complex forms of integration
- Shift in power within distribution channels from manufacturers to wholesalers and retailers
- Transparency, openness, availability of information
- Flexible manufacturing, inventory, logistical, and purchasing systems
- Speech-driven machines and products
- Value that derives from relationships, networks, extended alliances, and mosaics
- Interactivity, mobility, convertibility, connectivity, ubiquity, and globalization in communications

---

Source: Adaped from Naisbitt and Aburdene (1990) and Toffler (1990).

from anywhere in the world. Similarly, while companies can be expected to outsource all of their educational requirements, traditional public educational institutions may outsource most of their basic operations (including teaching, information technology, marketing, food service, janitorial service, grounds maintenance, fundraising). Opportunities for the entrepreneur abound.

CHANGING MARKETS, MARKETING, AND THE ENTREPRENEUR

Of all the changes underway, perhaps the most significant from the entrepreneur's point of view concern customers and markets. The entrepreneur's ultimate accountability is to the customer, without whom there is no venture (start-up or corporate). Creating value for a customer and developing a sustainable relationship are the building blocks to achieving competitive advantage.

Developments in technology, demographics, standards of living, information availability, deregulation, social mores, and the intensity of competition have all combined to dramatically affect how markets must be defined and approached. The future success of entrepreneurs will depend on their ability to capitalize on the revolution taking place in markets and, by extension, in marketing.

Only a few years ago, the core problem in many organizations was to move from thinking of marketing as selling to approaching marketing as a set of value-creating activities that are captured in the so-called marketing mix (product, price, promotion, and distribution). Today, the problem is much more complicated. Figure 10.1 illustrates three related trends in the ongoing evolution of marketing practice.

In essence, the left-hand column in Figure 10.1 suggests that the mass market is dead. From hotels to beers to publishing to financial services to structural steel, market after market is fragmented, segmented, and niched. Consider ath-

Figure 10.1
Three Different Ways in Which Markets and Marketing Approaches Are Evolving

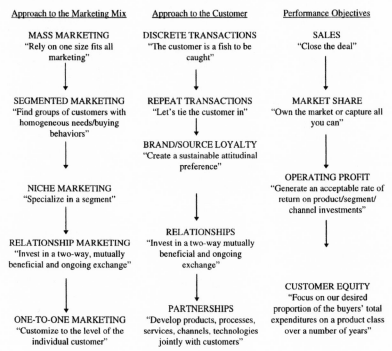

Approach to the Marketing Mix	Approach to the Customer	Performance Objectives
MASS MARKETING "Rely on one size fits all marketing"	DISCRETE TRANSACTIONS "The customer is a fish to be caught"	SALES "Close the deal"
SEGMENTED MARKETING "Find groups of customers with homogeneous needs/buying behaviors"	REPEAT TRANSACTIONS "Let's tie the customer in"	MARKET SHARE "Own the market or capture all you can"
	BRAND/SOURCE LOYALTY "Create a sustainable attitudinal preference"	
NICHE MARKETING "Specialize in a segment"		OPERATING PROFIT "Generate an acceptable rate of return on product/segment/channel investments"
RELATIONSHIP MARKETING "Invest in a two-way, mutually beneficial and ongoing exchange"	RELATIONSHIPS "Invest in a two-way mutually beneficial and ongoing exchange"	
ONE-TO-ONE MARKETING "Customize to the level of the individual customer"	PARTNERSHIPS "Develop products, processes, services, channels, technologies jointly with customers"	CUSTOMER EQUITY "Focus on our desired proportion of the buyers' total expenditures on a product class over a number of years"

letic shoes (once called sneakers or tennis shoes). In times past, a consumer went to the shoe department in a department store, or to a shoe store, and had a choice between black and white, high-top or low-top. Today, he/she goes to an athletic shoe store and has 60 or 70 shoe types to select from, one for every type of athletic activity and type of foot, with numerous features to choose from as well (e.g., color, air pump, lace versus velcro).

Increasingly, the entrepreneur must segment the market, prioritize one or two key segments to be targeted, and tailor the marketing mix (i.e., the product or service offering, the price charged, the communications approach, and the distribution channel or method) to each segment. Further, entrepreneurs will often specialize in serving a single segment, or niche. Beyond this is relationship marketing, where the firm makes unique investments in individual customer accounts, interacts closely with them, and tailors aspects of the marketing mix. The ultimate step is where the firm engages in one-to-one marketing and tailors the entire marketing mix to individual accounts. Business-to-business marketers have done this for years (e.g., IBM when it deals with NASA or Ford Motor Company), but increasingly innovative consumer marketers are engaging in one-to-one marketing. A case in point is Lands End, the highly successful and very entrepreneurial direct marketing company. It is able to customize aspects of the product (e.g., a man's shirt with a personal monogram), quote a unique price, have highly personalized communication, and quickly deliver the product to the customer's front door using express delivery services.

A second evolution involves what one is trying to achieve vis-à-vis the customer. The traditional concern has been the "one-time or single occasion" transaction. Increasingly, however, survival requires that firms develop groups of attitudinally and behaviorally loyal customers, or that they establish formal relationships, or perhaps even that they partner with customers in developing new technologies, products, or logistical approaches.

The third evolution concerns how the entrepreneur measures performance. Sales revenue and market share were the old gods. Today, however, the concern is more with the profitability of individual segments and customers. The move is on, though, to focusing on the "lifetime value" of a customer and setting a goal for how much of their expenditure in a particular product category the entrepreneur wants to capture over that lifetime (or a strategically relevant time period). This is called customer equity. Thus, Land's End might set a goal of capturing 40% of your total clothing expenditures over the next ten years.

Let's consider the entrepreneur who has purchased a gas station and upgraded it to also include a quick lube and quick tune service center. Significant opportunity can be discovered by doing an assessment of the current customer base. Assume that two of the major sub-groups identified include (1) passing tourists who stop in for gas, but who are not from the area and are unlikely to return; and (2) local residents on the way to or from work. The first group are managed as one-off transactions, where quality service is the rule, but the ultimate goal is to maximize revenue per transaction. The second group is typified by Ms.

Jones, a local accountant who is well-established in the community. In her case, the entrepreneur has a potential relationship. The question becomes What proportion of Ms. Jones's total gasoline and auto maintenance expenditures over the next seven years do I want to capture? Our entrepreneur might get creative, offering Ms. Jones a special attractively-priced package. Suppose he offers to pick her car up at her place of work on the first Wednesday of every other month, bring it to the station, change all the lubricants, do a quick tune-up, wash and wax the car, and return it before the end of the workday? He also offers her credit, regular specials, and a log that includes detailed information on her car, its condition, what he has done to it, and when. Finally, he communicates with her personally through monthly mailings that cover such topics as when to use which fuels, how to use less gas when driving, future price trends, and when to start looking for a new car.

Movement along each of the evolutionary paths pictured in Figure 10.1 results in the entrepreneur's marketing efforts becoming:

- more intense,
- more focused,
- more expensive,
- more complex, and
- requiring more hard work.

Essentially, we are saying that the entrepreneur will have to become more of a marketer, and as a marketer, he/she will have to be more of an entrepreneurial marketer.

What then, is meant by the term "entrepreneurial marketing"? It is an opportunistic perspective wherein the marketer is not simply responsible for communication activities but instead, must continually discover new sources of value for customers. Value is created through unique combinations within the marketing mix. The entrepreneurial marketer challenges the assumptions and conventional wisdom that prevail in a given industry. He/she strives to lead customers rather than follow them.

As markets and marketing approaches evolve, the challenge to the entrepreneur will be to uncover distinct market segments and niches, while finding ways to customize the marketing mix down to the level of the market segment and the individual account. He/she must also learn to estimate the lifetime value of a customer and then determine the appropriate levels and types of investments to be made in individual accounts. All of this implies the need for keen insight into customer lifestyles or operations and (often unstated or unperceived) customer needs, and into the changing trade-offs that customers are willing to make among core product, service, and vendor attributes. The entrepreneurial marketer becomes a creative consultant, helping customers adapt to a discontinuous future.

It also suggests that entrepreneurs will have to develop and continually update highly detailed (and often interactive) customer databases. In this conceptualization, the most important element of the marketing mix is not *promotion*, it becomes *product (or service)*. The entrepreneur will find it necessary to produce a continual stream of new lines, additions to lines, product and service improvements or revisions, new applications, and repositioning efforts. At the same time process innovation will be vital. This will include new approaches to segmentation, pricing, use of the brand, packaging, customer credit, logistics, design and management of distribution channels, database management, customer communication, and management of customer service levels.

ENTREPRENEURIAL DILEMMAS AND THE FUTURE

George Gilder (1988, p. 49) indicates that "It is the entrepreneurs who know the rules of the world and the laws of God. Thus they sustain the world—they overthrow establishments rather than establish equilibria." Gilder is certainly correct in his characterization of the "entrepreneur as hero," which is the conventional stereotype. Yet, not all entrepreneurs produce dramatic breakthroughs. Ironically, those who do overthrow the establishment frequently find that the returns they achieve can be less than those received by less ambitious entrepreneurs.

This is one of a number of fundamental dilemmas confronting those interested in entrepreneurship. As entrepreneurship plays a more pronounced role in the lives of individuals, organizations, and societies, it is crucial that dilemmas such as these be recognized, and that strategies be developed for addressing them. Below, we have identified five critical dilemmas and some of the issues surrounding each of them.

The Dilemma of Risk versus Return

The relationship between what an entrepreneur does and the outcomes or returns achieved is not a simple one. It is often assumed that major breakthroughs, or higher risk ventures, generate higher returns. But this is not always the case, as returns are influenced by timing, managerial competence, market conditions, and a host of environmental factors. Even if one controls for all of these factors though, doing something that is highly entrepreneurial only raises the possible ceiling on returns if one is successful. Actual returns are unique to the venture.

We believe that the general level of risk facing any entrepreneur will increase in the coming years simply because more entrepreneurship will be occurring. Within this broader context, the probability of failure will be higher for those individuals, organizations, and societies who pursue both very low and very high levels of entrepreneurial intensity (EI). We further believe that the highest returns will come to those who can sustain a balance of degree and frequency of entrepreneurship over time.

The Dilemma of the Individual versus the Team

Entrepreneurship requires a visionary individual with drive and commitment. Entrepreneurship also requires a dedicated team of specialists and generalists. The problem becomes one of emphasizing both individualism and collective teamwork at the same time. Unfortunately, a policy or procedure that incentivizes individual action can serve as a disincentive for collective action. Similarly, a preoccupation with teams will come at the expense of entrepreneurial leadership. Achieving a balance can be tricky.

Nonetheless, in an age of multiple careers and lessened organizational loyalty, the entrepreneur will have to be less of a team dictator and more of a team member. He/she will have to share ownership and control with team members. The objective will be to build an organization based on core competencies and to focus on the continued development of knowledge assets that can deliver these competencies. Thus, the internal team itself becomes fluid or subject to change.

The Dilemma of the Self-Contained Unit versus the Network

As we enter an age where large organizations find that small truly is beautiful, a premium will be placed on being flexible and fast. At the same time, the competitive advantage of small entrepreneurial firms vis-à-vis large corporations will dissipate as the large corporates downsize, restructure, and reengineer. The entrepreneur who is building a venture will need to focus less on accumulating assets and achieving control through ownership and more on building a fluid, adaptable organization that is highly leveraged in terms of financing, buildings, equipment, administrative services, and staffing.

Perhaps the best way to express this is that entrepreneurs will have to think individually, but act collectively. That is, they will best be able to achieve market power through external alliances and networks, not by acquisition or an increase in their physical asset base.

They will effectively gain control by giving up control. Further, external commitments will not be permanent, as individual members of a dynamic network come and go. A new form of barter will arise in terms of what different organizations have to offer to one another in exchange for cooperation.

The Dilemma of Stability versus Turbulence

Entrepreneurship requires both stability and instability. Where there is an established environmental infrastructure (e.g., financial institutions, utilities, transport, distribution channels, courts, police), entrepreneurship is facilitated. Yet, environmental turbulence (e.g., regulatory, technological, market-related, competitive) creates opportunities for proactive entrepreneurs. In fact, there is a circle of turbulence, in that environmental turbulence gives rise to entrepreneurial opportunity, and entrepreneurial behavior in turn produces disruption, or more environmental turbulence. Politicians and economists seem concerned that this cycle will spin out of control, such that unfettered growth will result in rampant inflation and economic chaos. Yet, there is little evidence to support their fears. Periods of uncontrolled inflation and economic instability have typically been the result of far too little entrepreneurial activity, not too much.

There is a related dilemma here, in that entrepreneurship is both constructive and destructive. Entrepreneurs create the new, and in doing so, they preemptorily make existing products, services, and processes obsolete. The copier can still make good copies when it is replaced by a quicker, better machine. In the future, this creative destruction will accelerate, as entrepreneurs find they must continually make their own products obsolete. Along the way, whole new entrepreneurial opportunities will be created for recycling, retrofitting, and identifying alternative distribution channels (reaching new markets) for the products being displaced.

The Dilemma of Success versus Failure

Although it is popular to talk about winners and losers, sustained entrepreneurship is not that simple. Entrepreneurs are often competitive, with a need to win. They are replacing conventional managers who have a need to avoid failure. Yet, many entrepreneurs fail. A considerable number of well-known entrepreneurs experienced failure before ever achieving success. Others can describe an entire portfolio of successes and failures, where one solid hit is followed by a strikeout and two ground outs, and then a home run.

Within failure are the seeds of success. Entrepreneurs must increasingly believe in the successful failure, where lessons from unsuccessful efforts are used to adapt one's concepts and ideas into something that will work. This is important on two levels. A general increase in new product and service introductions and new venture start-ups by definition means a higher failure rate. Similarly, as individuals find themselves doing more entrepreneurial things in their own lives, they will also begin to fail more often. Success will increasingly be a function of one's ability to overcome the psychological fear or avoidance of failure that is ingrained in virtually all of us.

TOMORROW'S ENTREPRENEURS

Given all that has been said about the future, will tomorrow's entrepreneur differ from his/her contemporary counterpart? On some basic issues, one would expect few differences. Entrepreneurs as a group will tend to share certain characteristics (e.g., achievement motivation, internal locus of control, calculated risk-taking). Entrepreneurs as a group will remain passionate about their venture and will be opportunity-driven. As Schwartz (1988, p. 32) has noted, "When the cash register starts ringing, the businessperson feels happy—the entrepreneur feels bored." This will not change. Entrepreneurs as a group will continue to demonstrate significant diversity among their ranks, with a number of different types of entrepreneurs emerging.

However, some changes are also likely. We not only believe that there will be more entrepreneurs, but that all of us will have to find ways to introduce more entrepreneurship into our lives. This means that the pool of entrepreneurs will grow significantly, become even more diverse, and that new categories or new types of entrepreneurs will emerge. The new categories will describe subsets of entrepreneurs found not only in commerce, but in all walks of life.

Other changes are probable as well. Levinson (1997) provides a somewhat normative picture of the future entrepreneur that centers around the concept of balance (e.g., between demands of the venture and one's personal lifestyle, or between company financial performance and a sense of organizational learning and value creation). Table 10.4 includes an outline of Levinson's conceptualization of the twenty-first century entrepreneur.

Our own view is that, in spite of their growing diversity, entrepreneurs will share some additional commonalities. Significantly, we will see the emergence of:

- *The Global Entrepreneur*—There will be a greater awareness of what is happening in other parts of the world, and entrepreneurs will more quickly adapt to or adopt approaches used by others. Entrepreneurs will also focus increasingly on global sources of supply and global markets for their own products. This will be chiefly accomplished through networks and alliances.
- *The Ethically and Environmentally Conscious Entrepreneur*—Tomorrow's entrepreneurs will define high ethical standards as a key factor in their long-term performance. They will develop a keen sense of their own ethical standards and those of their employees, and these standards will be based on consistent rather than situational behavior guidelines. Similarly, entrepreneurs will be conscious not simply of resource efficiency but of the environmental externalities that result from their businesses. This awareness will include the raw material inputs they use; the disposal or recycling of their unused outputs and waste; the appearance of their physical facilities, equipment, vehicles, and signage; the noise that they generate; and related side-effects of their operations.
- *The Technologically Competent Entrepreneur*—The entrepreneur will understand that technology goes beyond knowing how to turn on his/her own personal computer. As knowledge becomes the key competency, and competitive advantage comes more from speed, adaptability and aggressiveness, the entrepreneur will stress extensive process innovation as new user-friendly technologies are integrated into all aspects of the venture's operations.
- *The Lifestyle-Conscious Entrepreneur*—Raised in a time of relative world peace, limited nuclear threat, global economic growth, free trade, general affluence, and environ-

Table 10.4
The Twenty-First Century Entrepreneur: A Normative View

_____

In the future, entrepreneurs will:

• emphasize balance between the demands or sacrifices of work and the freedom for leisure and lifestyle;

• pursue opportunities based on work that makes him/her happy; will be passionate about the work, while recognizing that the journey is the goal;

• be more concerned with profitability, vitality, quality, learning, and value than growth or size;

• proceed at a steady, planned pace; will work according to a plan; will view stress as an indicator of an unplanned or incorrect approach;

• be disciplined, focused on the task at hand, and concerned more with today than yesterday or tomorrow; will be focused on business strategy as well;

• be team players, dependent upon many others, with an appreciation for mutual dependency;

• emphasize the linking of his/her business to other synergistic enterprises, in the process leveraging resources; as a rule these linkages are not permanent, and many are shorter-term;

• focus on both internal and external flexibility and adaptability.

_____

Source: Adaped from Levinson (1997).

mentalism, tomorrow's entrepreneur will be conscious of quality of life (QOL) considerations. He/she will find ways to enhance QOL through his/her ventures (e.g., working from home or remote locations, creating more holistic work environments that address such issues as daycare, stress on the job, and flextime). He/she will also be more conscious of the value of a private life, time off, adventurous travel, and family and civic involvement.

• *The Multiple Venture Entrepreneur*—The norm for tomorrow's entrepreneur will be a series of entrepreneurial ventures over their lives, and a tendency to have their fingers in multiple ventures at one time. Some of these ventures may have short life spans; others may be ongoing. Stated differently, then, the individual's average EI score will rise, especially in terms of the frequency dimension.

With this last point, we are suggesting a growing emphasis on lifelong entrepreneurship. To truly realize the potential of entrepreneurship as a philosophy, objective, strategy, attitude, and behavioral process—in short, as a source of sustainable advantage—it has to be applied over the entire life cycles of people, organizations, and societies.

TOWARD SUSTAINABLE ADVANTAGE: ENTREPRENEURSHIP AND LIFE CYCLES

The concept of EI is based on the fundamental principle that individuals, organizations, and societies differ in terms of the number of entrepreneurial events they pursue, and the degree to which those events are innovative, involve calculated risks, and are proactive. In Chapter 4, we illustrated the EI concept by showing where a particular person, company, or country might fall in the entrepreneurial grid. In essence, we were assessing entrepreneurial performance at a point in time, or over a finite period of time, such as the past two years.

In the years ahead, we will witness a shift in emphasis toward lifelong entrepreneurship. The concern will be less with achieving something entrepreneurial at one point in one's career or in the life of a company, and more with sustaining it on an ongoing basis. In addition, we will see the role of entrepreneurs change as life cycles evolve.

A life cycle approach attempts to identify major phases of development in the life of a person, product, company, technology, political movement, or national economy. In this book, we have focused upon individuals, organizations, and societies. The developmental life cycle of each are illustrated in Figure 10.2.

The Individual's Life Cycle

Consider the individual. As people evolve through the stages of their lives, changes occur in the relative importance they place on such factors as acceptance, security, materialism, experimentation, structure, diversity, personal

Figure 10.2
Individual, Organizational, and Societal Life Styles

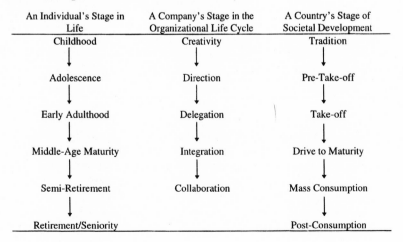

An Individual's Stage in Life	A Company's Stage in the Organizational Life Cycle	A Country's Stage of Societal Development
Childhood	Creativity	Tradition
↓	↓	↓
Adolescence	Direction	Pre-Take-off
↓	↓	↓
Early Adulthood	Delegation	Take-off
↓	↓	↓
Middle-Age Maturity	Integration	Drive to Maturity
↓	↓	↓
Semi-Retirement	Collaboration	Mass Consumption
↓		↓
Retirement/Seniority		Post-Consumption

achievement, partnering, family, roots, and privacy (cf. Sheehy, 1976). The relative importance of frequency versus degree of entrepreneurship is also likely to change as one moves through the stages in Figure 10.2. Selling lemonade in front of one's home as a child and organizing school dances as an adolescent might give way to a period of apprenticeship with an established company, where one experiments with modest process innovations. This might be followed by a period where one champions major innovation within the firm, participates in a business start-up on the side, or simply breaks away and goes it alone. The first independent venture might be followed by participation in a second or third. Later in life, one might help champion social innovation in terms of novel solutions to a problem in the local church or within the community.

Of course, any number of patterns can emerge. By early adulthood, however, one would expect that the individual had begun to develop some semblance of a strategy for entrepreneurship. Also, the relative emphasis on entrepreneurship in one's professional versus family versus social lives can be expected to change over time. For instance, social experimentation might be more in evidence during adolescent and semi-retirement years, while professional experimentation might come more during early adulthood, and again in semi-retirement.

The Organizational Life Cycle

If we turn to the corporation and its organizational life cycle, analogous patterns might emerge. Companies typically start out as fairly creative and entrepreneurial entities. However, the need for controls and structures becomes critical once a certain size is achieved. The organization subsequently evolves through stages, which are disrupted by periodic crises. These crises are addressed over time by alternating between such strategies as delegation or centralization; and the formation of autonomous business units, integrative superstructures, or matrix teams (see Adizes, 1978; Griener, 1972). To address the various crises and organizational requirements that arise, ongoing changes occur in the managerial focus, company structure, leadership style, control system, reward policies, and corporate culture. However, these changes also tend to systematically undermine (or lead to a de-emphasis on) entrepreneurship.

An alternative approach is to strategically manage entrepreneurship, identifying different roles for it, and approaches to it, depending on the stage in the organizational life cycle. Not only will the relative importance of degree and frequency differ over time, but so too will the priority given to product versus service versus process innovation. So, too, might one expect the extent to which entrepreneurship comes from the top, the bottom, or the middle of the company to vary. Further, as a company evolves from being product-driven to production-driven to sales-driven to cost-driven to market-driven, the functional areas within the firm (such as production, research and development, sales, marketing, and finance) that lead the entrepreneurial change can be expected to alternate.

The Societal Life Cycle

Finally, let us briefly examine the ways in which societies evolve. There might first be a pre-development period characterized by a pastoral or nomadic existence. Next would come a stage where society is agriculturally-based, with limited access to technology and a hierarchical social structure based on family and clan. This would be followed by a period of initial (labor-intensive) industrialization and urbanization, which then would become more capital-intensive, with a focus on economies of scale and learning effects. Eventually, society would evolve to a more service-based, and then to a technology-based and knowledge-based foundation (Rostow, 1971; Toffler, 1990).

An interesting parallel perspective can be found in the work of Sirgy and Fox-Mangleberg (1988), who describe societal development in terms of a needs hierarchy. The initial concern is with survival needs, then safety needs, social needs, esteem needs, and finally, self-actualization needs. As societies advance up the hierarchy of needs, the focus changes from a production orientation, to a selling orientation, to a customer-satisfaction orientation, to a societal benefits orientation.

Entrepreneurship not only plays a unique role in each stage of societal evolution, but general levels of entrepreneurial intensity can determine how long a country stays in a particular stage as well as the overall pace of advancement through the various stages. Early stages might find an emphasis on the immigrant as entrepreneur, where much of the entrepreneurial behavior concerns small start-ups (shopkeepers, artisans, brickmakers) and the development of a merchant class. Subsequently, a number of visionary entrepreneurs contribute to a major leap forward by building critical infrastructure (e.g., banks; railroads; core industries such as steel, mining, or automobiles). Later, the entrepreneurs pioneer service innovation (e.g., hotels, package delivery, entertainment) and franchise systems (e.g., fast food, quick copy). This is followed by technology innovations (e.g., computer systems, robotics, lasers, biotechnology). Of course, in every stage one finds shopkeepers, infrastructure pioneers, service innovations, and inventors. However, it is the dominant entrepreneurial focus in any one stage that ultimately defines that stage.

One might further hypothesize that, as societies evolve, there is a change in conceptualization from the entrepreneur as every man (or woman), to the entrepreneur as bold hero, to the entrepreneur as every man (or woman). In a similar vein, early stages might find society preoccupied with frequency of entrepreneurship, the take-off stage with degree of entrepreneurship, and later stages with a balance of frequency and degree.

Lessons can be learned about sustained societal entrepreneurship from the experiences of South Korea, Singapore, and Chile in the latter part of the twentieth century (see Chapter 8). Each country has accelerated its movement through the developmental stages over a 30-year period. Each vividly illustrates both a heightened need and evolving role for entrepreneurship and enlightened government. As a case in point, Singapore initially concentrated on local entrepreneurs to start and grow labor-intensive manufacturing and export businesses. However, this rapidly evolved into an emphasis on technopreneurs, who run world-class, technology-based ventures. The key, of course, is entrepreneurial government, which charts a long-term strategy for societal entrepreneurship.

CONCLUSIONS

These are exciting times to be alive, just as they are very trying times. The competitive environment is hostile and threatening, but it is also filled with opportunity. We live in an age of conflict, turbulence, and paradox. It is an era that can be characterized in many ways, but most importantly, it is the age of entrepreneurship.

We are witnessing what might be called the "democratization of entrepreneurship." Entrepreneurs have always come from all walks of life and pursued all types of ventures. Entrepreneurship is indifferent to race, religion, or age, although some societies have put up discriminatory barriers to certain people doing entrepreneurial things. Yet, in spite of all this, those who actually pursue entrepreneurial ventures have historically represented an extremely small percentage of the total population. This percentage is rapidly increasing and will increase even more in the coming years. Further, in one way or another, entrepreneurship will play an active role in virtually everyone's life.

In this final chapter, we have looked at where emerging opportunities might lie in the new millennium for those who act on their entrepreneurial impulses, and how entrepreneurs themselves can be expected to change. Fundamental dilemmas in the phenomenon of entrepreneurship were identified. The central concept though is the notion of lifetime entrepreneurship. There is a need for individuals, organizations, and societies to develop strategies for managing entrepreneurship over their life cycles. The most common two words in our daily vocabularies must become, what if.

The subtitle of this book contains the words "sustainable advantage." To sustain is to give strength to, encourage, keep from falling, or keep going continuously. Advantage refers to a position that gives one precedence, favorable circumstance, or superiority. Entrepreneurship is the source of strength that allows individuals to continuously put themselves into favorable circumstances, regardless of how unfavorable the surrounding conditions are. It enables companies to move quicker, be more nimble, and arrive in places before customers or competitors have been there. It changes the standard by which societies judge themselves, raising the sights and expectations of all citizens. In modern times, entrepreneurial intensity becomes the compass that will take us to a future of unlimited possibilities, newfound freedoms, and enhanced life satisfaction for every member of the human family.

REFERENCES

Adizes, I. 1978. "Organizational Passages—Diagnosing and Treating Lifecycle Problems of Organizations." *Organizational Dynamics* (Summer), 2–25.

Gilder, G. 1988. "The Revitalization of Everything: The Law of the Microcosm." *Harvard Business Review*, 66 (March–April), 49–61.

Griener, L.E. 1972. "Evolution and Resolution as Organizations Grow." *Harvard Business Review*, 50 (July–August), 37–46.

Handy, C. 1989. *The Age of Unreason.* London: Arrow Books.

Handy, C. 1994. *The Empty Raincoat.* London: Arrow Books.

Hawken, P. 1978. *Growing a Business.* New York: Fireside.

Levinson, J.C. 1997. *The Way of the Guerrilla.* Boston: Houghton Mifflin.

Naisbitt, J. 1994. *Global Paradox.* New York: William Morrow and Co.

Naisbitt, J., and Aburdene, P. 1990. *Megatrends 2000.* New York: William Morrow & Co.

Popcorn, F. 1991. *The Popcorn Report.* New York: Doubleday.

Popcorn, F., and Marigold, L. 1996. *Clicking.* New York: HarperCollins.

Robertson, P. 1996. *The New Millennium.* Dallas: World Publishing.

Rostow, N.W. 1971. *The Stages of Economic Growth.* New York: Cambridge University Press.

Schwartz, B. 1988. "Betting on Yourself." *Lear's* (March–April), 43–44.

Sheehy, G. 1976. *Passages: Predictable Crises of Adult Life.* New York: E.P. Dutton.

Sirgy, M.H., and Fox-Mangleberg, T. 1988. "Toward a General Theory of Social System Development: A Management/Marketing Perspective." *Systems Research*, 5 (2), 115–30.

Toffler, A. 1990. *Power Shift.* New York: Bantam Books.

Suggested Readings

Adizes, I. 1988. *Corporate Lifecycles: How and Why Corporations Grow and Die*. Englewood Cliffs, NJ: Prentice-Hall.

Bird, B.J. 1989. *Entrepreneurial Behavior*. London: Scott, Foresman.

Bygrave, W.D. (ed.). 1977. *The Portable MBA in Entrepreneurship*. New York: John Wiley and Sons.

Bygrave, W.D. 1993. "Theory Building in the Entrepreneurship Paradigm." *Journal of Business Venturing*, 8 (3), 250–280.

Drucker, P. 1985. *Innovation and Entrepreneurship: Practices and Principles*. New York: Harper and Row.

Gartner, W.R. 1985. "A Conceptual Framework for Describing the Phenomenon of New Venture Creation." *Academy of Management Review*, 10 (4), 696–706.

Gartner, W.R. 1988. "Who Is the Entrepreneur? Is the Wrong Question." *American Journal of Small Business*, 12 (4), 33–39.

Gerber, M.E. 1986. *The E-Myth*. Cambridge, MA: Ballinger Publishing.

Gilder, G. 1988. "The Revitalization of Everything: The Law of the Microcosm." *Harvard Business Review*, 66 (March–April), 49–61.

Gilder, G. 1984. *The Spirit of Enterprise*. New York: Simon & Schuster.

Hamel, G., and Prahalad, C.K. 1991. "Corporate Imagination and Expeditionary Marketing." *Harvard Business Review*, 69 (July–August), 81–92.

Hawken, P. 1987. *Growing a Business*. New York: Fireside.

Hisrich, R.D. 1986. *Entrepreneurship, Intrapreneurship and Venture Capital*. Lexington: Lexington Books.

Hood, J., and Young, E. 1993. "Entrepreneurship's Requisite Areas of Development: A Survey of Top Executives in Entrepreneurial Firms." *Journal of Business Venturing*, 8 (2), (March), 115–136.

McMillan, I.C., Block, Z., and Narasimha, P.N.S. 1986. "Corporate Venturing: Alternatives, Obstacles Encountered and Experience Effects." *Journal of Business Venturing*, 1 (2), 177–192.

Miner, J.B. 1996. *The Four Routes to Entrepreneurial Success.* San Francisco: Berrett-Koehler Publishers.

Pinchot III, G. 1985. *Intrapreneuring.* New York: Harper and Row.

Reynolds, P.D. 1987. "Organizations: Predicting Contributions and Survival." In R. Ronstadt et al. (eds.), *Frontiers of Entrepreneurship Research.* Wellesley, MA: Babson College, 584–609.

Roberts, E.B. 1991. *Entrepreneurs in High Technology: Lessons from MIT and Beyond.* New York: Oxford University Press.

Sexton, D.L. and Kasarda, J.D. (eds.). 1992. *The State of the Art of Entrepreneurship.* Boston: PWS-Kent.

Stefflre, V. 1985. "Organizational Obstacles to Innovation: A Formulation of the Problem." *Journal of Product Innovation Management*, 2, 3–11.

Stevenson, H., and Carlos, J. 1990. "A Paradigm of Entrepreneurship." *Strategic Management Journal*, 11, 17–27.

Stevenson, H., and Gumpert, D.E. 1985. "The Heart of Entrepreneurship." *Harvard Business Review*, 63 (March–April), 85–93.

Timmons, J.A. 1990. *New Venture Creation: Entrepreneurship in the 1990's.* Homewood, IL: Irwin Publishing.

Index

About the Author

MICHAEL MORRIS is currently Visiting Professor of Marketing at Georgetown University, after holding the position of Donald Gordon Professor of Entrepreneurship at the University of Cape Town, South Africa. Morris is a founder and Managing Director of PenteVision, an international consulting and executive development firm, and has been personally involved in two entrepreneurial start-ups. He is author of more than 60 articles published in academic journals and author or coauthor of three books, among them *Market-Oriented Pricing: Strategies for Management* (Quorum, 1990).